In memory of
Fr. Stan Bernacki

The Imitation of
St. Therese of the Child Jesus

The Imitation of St. Therese of the Child Jesus

by

Sf. Navantes

translated by
Sister Mary Grace, O.C.

FRANCISCAN HERALD PRESS
1434 WEST 51st STREET ● CHICAGO, 60609

The Imitation of St. Therese of the Child Jesus by S. Navantes, translated by Sister Mary Grace, O.C. from the French *L'Imitation de Sainte Therese de l'Enfant Jesus,* Desclee de Brouwer & Cie., 1929. Copyright © 1979 by Franciscan Herald Press, 1434 West 51st Street, Chicago, IL 60609.

Library of Congress Cataloging in Publication Data

Navantes, S
  The imitation of St. Therese of the Child of
Jesus.

  Translation of L'imitation de Sainte Therese de
l'Enfant Jesus.
    1. Thèrése, Saint, 1873–1897—Meditations.
 I. Title.
BX4700.T5N3213   242   79-1132
ISBN 0-8199-0764-2

NIHIL OBSTAT:
  Mark Hegener O.F.M.
  Censor
IMPRIMATUR:
  Msgr. Richard A. Rosemeyer, J.C.D.
  Vicar General, Archdiocese of Chicago
May 1, 1979

MADE IN THE UNITED STATES OF AMERICA

Contents

Preface   vii

Foreword   ix

Introduction   xiii

Chapter 1—Character Sketch—The Faults of Little Therese   1

Chapter 2—Her Faith   11

Chapter 3—Her Hope   23

Chapter 4—Her Love for God   33

Chapter 5—Her Charity Towards Her Neighbor   45

Chapter 6—Her Humility   59

Chapter 7—Her Spirit of Prayer   71

Chapter 8—Her Devotion to Our Lord Jesus Christ   87

Chapter 9—Her Devotion to the Blessed Mother   101

Chapter 10—Her Way of Spiritual Childhood   115

Chapter 11—Her Sufferings   131

Chapter 12—Her Monastic Virtues   149

Chapter 13—Her Prudence in the Direction of Souls   167

Chapter 14—Her Last Illness—Her Death   187

Epilogue   203

Act of Oblation to Merciful Love   207

Little Flower's Days of Grace   211

Preface

This little volume was first put into my hands many years ago by one of my Sisters here at the Middletown Carmel who knew of my personal deep devotion to Little Therese, and who—like me—wanted to see this work translated into English.

Originally, this book was meant simply to be used as edification for our own Sisters in Carmel; but when the work was completed, the Sisters here in Middletown suggested that it be published so that we might share with others these pages on the beautiful interior life of our little Carmelite Sister.

We reasoned that, as Carmelites, we must not keep the "secrets of the King" to ourselves, but rather share them so that, indeed, St. Therese's prophecy can be further extended: "All the world will love me."

We are convinced that to know Therese is to love her. This book is so arranged that each Chapter dwells on some one of her specific virtues through her childhood until her death; in a sense, this book is autobiographical. Even her "weaknesses" are not hidden here, but because of the virtue she practiced these very weaknesses redound to her glory. We get to know Therese through these pages; and knowing her, we love her.

This book was a labor of love for the translator; a work completed by snatching odd moments out of a daily busy schedule. It is a work shared by many persons who, like the author and the translator, feel a special affinity to St. Therese.

vii

Mother Teresa, O. Carm., R.I.P., was the real inspiration behind the first draft of this translation. Her spiritual conferences to us, as young religious, were often based on this little book translating it as she went along. Later, her motherly advice and assistance encouraged its completion; and Father John Clark, O.C.D., well-known devotee of St. Therese, lent his expertise and gave invaluable help to the final draft of this English version.

The Sisters in Middletown have been no less thoughtful by their ready encouragement, understanding, patience and, I am sure, their prayer in helping to arrange this material.

This is a work which has reaped its own reward in the realization that one more book about St. Therese will serve to sing the glory and goodness of God by offering her to the world as a model of strength in weakness—even more, as an example worthy of our imitation as the title so obviously proclaims.

When Pope Pius XI canonized St. Therese, he called her "The star of my Pontificate." Not only is she the star of his Pontificate, but literally the star—the guiding light—of thousands of souls who can identify with her because of her littleness and her weakness: "O Jesus . . . if You should find a soul weaker than mine. . . . You would grant it still greater favors."

How the world needs someone who it can touch, with whom it can identify today! Truly, Therese is that twentieth-century saint; she never becomes outdated. And because of her ability to attract, her influence on souls will continue to reach far and wide through this century and into the next.

We feel privileged, through this translation, to have some share in delivering St. Therese's message to the English–speaking world, and to be the feeble instruments of God's almighty design, knowing well that "strength is made perfect in weakness."

Sr. Mary Grace, O.C.
Carmelite Sisters
Middletown, New York

Foreword

"I feel that I am about to enter into my rest. But I feel especially that my mission is about to begin, my mission of making God loved as I love Him, of giving my little way to wouls. If God answers my desires, my heaven will be spent on earth until the end of the word. Yes, I want to spend my heaven doing good on earth. This isn't impossible, since from the bosom of the beatific vision the angles watch over us."

We have frequently heard these words of St.Therese quoted by spiritual writers, preachers, and especially her own devoted friends. We must not forget, however, that they were spoken with a certain conviction only after Therese Martin, the little, unknown child of Lisieux, had succeeded in serving God with great fidelity, experiencing in her own life His tender care and His divine mercies. In spite of a great deal of suffering, and she herself said "these sufferings will be known only in heaven," she never lost her patience with God. Her love for Him was very deep and intense. It had characteristics about it which had to be made known to others.

It seems, then, that in the providential disposition of her very short life, God chose her to be a special teacher of the way He wants to be loved by us. "I feel that my mission is about to begin, *my mission of making God loved the way I love Him,* of giving my little way to souls." God seems to have implanted this desire in her at a very early age. Father Almire Pichon, the Jesuit priest who was spiritual director to her older sisters and a friend of Therese's father, testified at the beatification and canonization process for Therese, that he had heard her make a statement like this even before her entrance into the Carmelite monastery of Lisieux. He never questioned her on its meaning, evidently because he did not take her seriously. The fact remains, nonetheless, that she did have this desire at an early age, and undoubtedly it was the work of the Holy Spirit in her soul, regarding the future mission she was to be given. While other children had their dreams of becoming something when they grew up, little Therese had her dreams of doing good on earth after her death, of making God loved as she loved him.

This book, then, entitled: *The Imitation of St. Therese* is very timely. Even after all these years, and yet it isn't so long since the little Carmelite nun went into eternity, September 30, 1897, she is still very much with us. Her devotees are to be counted in the thousands throughout the world. The ones who will succeed in reading it quietly and meditatively will find that St. Therese still has a message. The author has carefully chosen certain virtues practised by Therese, showing us how she made them part of her life, and then he gives us a practical application of their practice in our own day-to-day existence. To make the application is what is most necessary, for it is in the practice of virtue that the Christian life is lived out and that sanctity is gradually acquired. True, we may not be as strong as little Therese became, but at least we can try. We can be assured that the little Saint will aid us in our efforts.

St. Therese of the Child Jesus desired very much to be especially associated with all those whom she has chosen to call "little souls." She wrote in the "Story of a Soul," her autobiography:

"O Jesus! why can't I tell all little souls how unspeakable is your condescension? I feel that if You found a soul weaker and littler than mine—which is impossible—You would be pleased to grant it still greater favors, provided it abandoned itself with total confidence to Your Infinite Mercy. But why do I desire to communicate Your secrets of Love, O Jesus, for was it not You alone Who taught them to me, and can You not reveal them to others? Yes, I know it, and I beg You to do it. I beg you to cast your Divine Glance upon a great number of little souls. I beg you to choose a legion of little Victims worthy of Your LOVE!"

By the term "little souls" Therese means those who suffer from their miseries, their failures, their weakness, and their natural incapacity to practice virtue. She desired to be closely associated with all souls of this type. She desired very much, too, to be identified with all those who are unimportant, unknown, insignificant, enjoying no esteem and consideration of those with whom they come in contact. Her love goes out to those who struggle without any consolation, whose courage is at a low ebb when striving to carry out their destiny as human beings and children of God.

Let us not fail, then, to call upon this little Saint, begging her to extend a helpful hand to us in our daily struggle to love God and become His faithful children. Her hand has become very strong, for now it shares in the very power of God himself, whom she served so well on earth that she dared to say before her death: "God will have to do my will in heaven because I never did my will when I was on earth."

John Clarke, O.C.D.
Institute of Carmelite Studies
Washington, D.C.

Introduction

Pius XI called St. Therese the star of his pontificate. It is because of his veneration for her that this work was written.

Giving inspiration, he said, "It has pleased God to make known throughout the world the perfect practice of Spiritual Childhood in which, simply and purely, Therese shows herself to be a master." And on the day of her canonization he pronounced, "We ardently desire that all the faithful of Christ become worthy to share in an abundant effusion of graces through the intercession of 'little Therese,' but we desire still more that they meditate on her attentively with a view to imitating her."

So this series of meditations has been written with the desire of the Sovereign Pontiff in mind, bringing into focus this devotion to St. Therese.

While there are already numerous edifying works about St. Therese of the Child Jesus, there are few meditations properly speaking.

Note, too, that there is an essential difference between reading and prayer. The one merely touches the soul while the other penetrates it intimately. In meditation the soul is enlightened, the will enflamed and steeped in love, like iron on the anvil under repeated blows.

If we meditate seriously on Therese instead of simply reading her, she will so powerfully influence us that we will be drawn to imitate her virtue. When this happens Jesus Christ will begin to dwell in us, will become the object of our contemplation. We need have no fear of being separated from Him in striving to imitate his virginal spouse.

St. Therese shows us a sure way to the union with God—the way she so effectively followed.

When one imitates Therese, one walks the footsteps of Jesus. Pius XI pointed out Therese's likeness to Christ, saying, "Whoever venerates Therese, venerates at the same time the Divine Model Whose likeness she bore."

It is doubtful that Therese ever thought of her work, written or otherwise, as a classical treatise of perfection. It was rather the simple outpouring of a childlike soul entrusting herself through obedience to her mother.

Her narrative is one of inexpressible simplicity and grace, leaving with the reader a most tender impression. But when the reader tries to imitate her, he/she often bogs down with analysis, complicating matters. Others imitate St. Therese of the Child Jesus only haphazardly.

It is to counter both of these extremes that we have written a methodical and formal *Imitation* of St. Therese.

A good general marshals his soldiers before battle, making a plan of attack. It must be the same for souls of good will enrolled in the spiritual legion of St. Therese.

In his day, St. Paul did not approve of beating the air nor risking one's life without intending to win the prize.[1] Let us profit by this thought, so the work of the *Imitation* can be fruitful.

The plan for this treatise is that it will be a handbook rather than a biography, that it will draw inspiration from the works, spirit, and life of St. Therese.

At times we become personal, making use of frequent quotations, yet refraining from practical applications which are to be drawn from them.

We feel long dissertations superfluous in a work of this kind, since its development is reserved to the work of the Holy Spirit for those who meditate. We took pains to outline in as exact a manner as possible the supernatural aspect of the saint.

Though St. Therese of the Child Jesus might be universally

loved, she is not always understood. Some authors have misunderstood her sanctity because they have tried to fit her into their own idea of holiness.

Others, carried away by poetic inspiration, have idealized her to excess, reducing the simplicity of her childlike soul to utter childishness. Oppositely, others have tried to discredit her completely—this virgin to whom God has manifested something of his own infinite beauty.

In an effort to demonstrate her virtue, some authors have watered down the marvelous and ingenuous story of Therese without taking account that spiritual childhood is precisely the distinctive mark of her sanctity, the way she marked out for others her providential mission.

And so well-intentioned hands, though not always skillful, have taken the rose and stripped the leaves from its stem, leaving behind only thorns.

Undoubtedly, Therese did suffer much! Was there ever a saint canonized who didn't?

Is there any doubt that the sisters of Therese, privileged to live with her for twenty-four years, were more qualified than anyone to form an exact opinion about this servant of God? They all agreed that Therese was simple, 'a child of God' who practiced all virtues with an heroic strength, especially those virtues characterizing spiritual childhood.

No matter what is said of her, the humble Carmelite is and will remain Little Therese because it is the name she chose on her death bed to be invoked under.

This childlike spirit does not prevent her from being a saint in the eyes of God and man. Has not our Lord told us that "He who would be the least here below would be the greatest in the Kingdom of Heaven"?[2]

So will we be among those who are influenced by the charm of littleness? Otherwise, attracted by the grandeur of the world, we will find something more satisfying than heavenly contact with the amiable Therese of Lisieux.

Regarding the affections, admiration is a normal prelude to

love. Does not one always begin by admiring what, in the end, he loves? Because love is imitative, it makes those who love one another congenial.

A thorough study of the captivating personality of Therese will, unquestionably, fill us with admiration of her, eventually leading us to imitate her.

Although we are lowly compared to St. Therese, we still dare to hope that we will be drawn to admire, to love, to imitate, the angelic nun of Lisieux.

Because of her worldwide popularity, it is hoped that many devotees of Therese will make use of these meditations. However, it should be remembered that to imitate St. Therese of the Child Jesus is not the work of a month, or even a year, but of a lifetime.

We hope that divine grace will inspire the reader to persevere in this study and above all in its practice.

If at times the style is whimsical, even in spiritual matters, it does not mean sanctity is lacking. There is no form of sanctity that attracts more than that of Therese who promised to spend eternity doing good.

We admire the glory with which the Sovereign Pontiff clothed Therese on the day of her canonization. "The same God," he said, "who raised up giants of apostolic sanctity has formed within the confines of the cloister a masterpiece of perfect sanctity—this ever humble, ever little and ever virginal child."

Let us proceed now to study prayerfully this masterpiece of sanctity and engrave her in our hearts, so she may be our inspiration in the eager pursuit of holiness and our guide to glory. Amen.

Notes

1. The exact quotation can be found in I Cor. 9:24-26.
2. Matthew 18:3-4.

Chapter One
Character Sketch—The Faults of Little Therese

Love is so powerful in its works
That it knows how to draw profit from everything—
The good as well as the bad which it finds in me
And transforms my soul into itself.

St. John of the Cross

What! Discredit Little Therese!

Be assured this humble saint would be the first to smile and say, "Go ahead, bring out my faults. It is by struggle even to the point of the sword that I have gained victory. And this is what you must do if you too wish to conquer."

Therese was gifted and versatile. She was candid, energetic, intelligent, warm-hearted.

Nevertheless, good as she was, she did inherit the effects of original sin.

God, skillful goldsmith as he is, purified her in the crucible of his love until there was fashioned the masterpiece of grace which Holy Mother Church now honors on our altars.

Yet it is a fact that Therese was impulsive at times—much more excusable, we admit, in a child still lacking the use of reason.

At three months of age this mite of a child could already upset the whole family.

1

"Therese was not living with us at the time," wrote Madame Martin. "One Sunday, her nurse brought her here with her own four children about eleven-thirty just as we were sitting down to eat. She placed the babe in our arms and left for Mass.

"That was fine, but it's not what the little one wanted; she screamed her head off. The whole house was in an uproar. We had to send Louise [servant] out to tell Rose [nurse] to come right back after Mass instead of going shopping to buy her children shoes as she had planned.

"The nurse left in the middle of Mass and hurried back. I was vexed."[1]

A few days later Therese showed a positive attachment for her nurse.

Madame Martin wrote, "The nurse brought her in but she did not want to stay with us and went into a fit of crying when she did not see her. So Louise had to take her to the market-place where Rose was busy selling her butter; there was no other way of doing it.

"When she saw Rose, she began to laugh and never made another sound; and Rose kept her there with her until noon selling her butter with all the other good women. For my part, I cannot hold her for long without becoming very tired. She weighs fourteen pounds. As she grows older, she will be very graceful and very pretty."[2]

The eldest sister Marie began teaching Celine, another sister, at home. But in order to keep her pupil's attention she would not permit Therese—barely three years old—in the class room.

Fascinated, Therese's budding curiosity spurred her to continue playing as usual.

"One day," remembered Marie, "I saw her at the door of my room trying to open it, but she was still too little to turn the knob. I watched to see what she would do: Would she cry or call someone to help her? But no, she said nothing; in her powerlessness, she gave up and lay down at the threshold of the door.

"I told my mother about this little escapade and she said to me: 'You must not let her do that.'

"The next day, the same thing happened. 'Therese,' I said, 'you are hurting the little Jesus.' She looked at me attentively. She understood so well what it meant that never again did she repeat this little act."[3] God's love was already instilled in this child's tender soul, her trying to combat her childish faults.

It was customary for the family to take their "Benjamin" each Sunday to a part of Vespers. One Sunday, the visit was omitted. Therese began to cry. Suddenly, she ran out in a downpour of rain in the direction of the church.

Therese clung tenaciously to her devotions. One evening her mother said firmly, "It is late, you can say your prayers tomorrow." Therese fussed.

"To end the matter her father let her say some," recounted Madame Martin.[4] But he did not let her say them all.

Time passing, this self-will became more pronounced. "My little Celine is all for practicing virtue," says another letter. "But I don't know what to say about that little rascal, Therese! . . . it's hard to tell . . . she is yet so small and heedless.

"Therese is a very intelligent child, but not so sweet as her sister and certainly more obstinate. When she says 'no' nothing will make her change her mind. One could leave her in the cellar all day without getting her to say 'yes'; she would rather spend the night there than give in."

"I had still another fault," the servant of God later pointed out, "and that was a great self-love. Mama wanted to know how far my pride would take me, and so she said to me one day: 'Therese, if you kiss the ground, I'll give you a penny!'

"A penny! that would have been a fortune to me. However, my pride asserted itself, and standing erect I answered: 'No, Mama, I would rather not have the penny.'"

Despite her youth, Therese was not indifferent to her looks and dress. One day she was not dressed to her liking and thought, "How much prettier I would look with bare arms!"

Shrewd, quick, vivacious, she was always ready with some inimitable reply[5] Celine was pestering Madame Martin one day to take her on an excursion to the Pavillion. Therese, apparently oblivious to what was being said, played with a stick in a corner of the garden. Suddenly, she screamed at her sister, "Don't torment Papa so that he thinks he has to take us out everyday!"

Celine would have to tolerate other ill treatment from Therese.

"Mama," Therese would confess, "I gave Celine a push, and I hit her once, but I won't do it again."

Capriciousness also seemed to have been a sin of this "little rascal."

One morning she pretended to be asleep. When her mother called her, she pouted and hid under the covers, saying, "I don't want anyone to look at me!"

Madame Martin went downstairs. Soon, full of remorse, Therese came down in tears. "Mama," she cried, "I have been bad; forgive me!"

Another sister, Leonie, now too big to play with dolls, offered her toys to her little sisters.

Celine contented herself with a ball of yarn. But Therese carried off the basket, declaring, "I want it all!"

One day—doing what she liked best, swinging—her father passed by and called out, "Come and give me a kiss, little queen."

The little girl answered, "If you want it, come and get it yourself, papa!"

Madame Martin pretended not to hear, but Marie scolded her saying, "You naughty little girl to speak like that to your father!" Immediately, Therese came in the house echoing with her cries of contrition.

Another time Victoria was the butt of one of Therese's outbursts. The poor girl, refusing to give in to her younger sister, mystified Therese so that she recalled, "Then, at the height of indignation I got up and stamped my foot with all my might and cried: 'Victoria, you wicked thing!' ... After crying in anger, alas! I shed tears of repentance."

Psychological study of these episodes reveals tendencies of a proud character, domineering and hotheaded. But, the clear judgment of St. Therese of the Child Jesus was not deceived.

"With such a nature," she wrote later in her autobiography, "I have a clear idea of what I would be like if I had been reared by less virtuous parents. I would have become very wicked, and perhaps even lost my immortal soul.

"Happily, Jesus watched over me; he turned all my faults to my advantage; curbed early, they served to lead me on to perfection."

Like a soldier who learns to fight, Therese learned to conquer.

Her frankness was as courageous as spontaneous.

"As soon as she has committed the least fault," noted her mother, "everyone must know about it.

"'Hurry, tell papa that I tore the wallpaper,' she said; then she stood like a criminal waiting to be condemned. She has an idea in her little head that if she accuses herself she will be more readily forgiven."

Therese was not content with owning up to her faults. She wanted to repair the damage she had caused.

One day she broke a vase which her mother had given her. Quickly, as was her custom, she showed what had happened. Madame Martin showing displeasure, the little girl began to cry.

A moment later she went to her mother and said, "Don't feel badly, mama; when I get big enough to earn money I promise that I shall buy you another one."

Madame Martin said to Pauline, "So you see, I can hardly keep up with her!"[6]

Little Therese practiced renouncement at an early age. One means adapted to her youth did much to encourage this.

Marie had brought back from the Visitation a special chaplet with movable beads, helping one count one's acts of virtue. Therese and Celine accepted it enthusiastically, even practicing mortification in their play.

One day, the two girls talking loudly about this, a neighbor overheard. The neighbor inquired of the girls.[7]

"I already had a great command over all my actions," Therese said, "so I was accustomed not to complain whenever anyone took what belonged to me.

"When I was accused unjustly, I preferred to be silent rather than to excuse myself. In the end, it was necessary to tell me only once: 'You must not do that', and I no longer had the desire to do it."

At an age when other children hardly obey except when under constraint, our saint had already begun to obey God.

So it would be wrong to conclude from the preceding that Therese had an exceptionally difficult character. Apparently, Madame Martin somewhat exaggerated her sketches of Therese to make them more impressive.

Intimate notes of Mother Agnes of Jesus support this. "Therese and I were talking together about our childhood, and I recalled a reflection which my mother made while I was a boarding student at the Visitation of Le Mans.

" 'Nothing interests you, I see, except to receive news of your little sisters, Celine and Therese, and although I search my mind to find something new to write to you it is sometimes difficult.'

"I am sure," I added, "that mama exaggerated some of your childish faults in order to have something lively to write to me.

"She answered simply. 'I believe you are right; it is true though that even before the age of three it was not necessary to tell me a thing over and over again in order to correct me. A single kind word was enough to make me understand and be sorry for my faults.'"

These faults were not grave. They were simply human weaknesses from which even saints are not exempt. As scripture says, "The just man falls seven times a day." More often, her supposed imperfections were only first impulses which she soon brought under control.

"I would not be able to explain so well these unfortunate feelings of nature if I had not found them in myself," she said, describing the temptations of her novices later on.

Nevertheless, there is a difference between feeling and consent. Defects of character, when overcome, become merits. That is how the servant of God sees it.

"Our nature is there," Therese observed. "It is not given to us for nothing, but for the treasures it helps us to acquire, It is our 'daily bread.'"

With effort, the servant of God became an expert in sacrifice. In her childhood, she strung beads for Jesus. In her youth, she picked roses for him. It is the same gesture. Only the emphasis is different. In times past, she would cry while unstringing beads. Now she smiles while scattering roses.

"When I was a child," she confided, "I suffered from sadness; now I can relish the most bitter fruits in peace and joy."

The stronger the soul, the more complete its mastery. But there are still thorns. Because of their sharpness, the courageous saint was able to bring under control 'her proud and ardent nature.'

Toward the end of her life, Therese referred to Christmas night of 1886, dating her strongest move toward Christ.

"Today I was thinking about my past life, about the offering which I had made before at Christmas... and the words of praise addressed to Judith came to mind: 'You have acted with manly courage, and your heart is strengthened.'[8]

"Some souls will say: 'I have not the courage to make such a sacrifice.' But let them make the effort! God never refuses the first grace to begin; after that, the heart is strengthened and one goes on from victory to victory."

As one can see, St. Therese of the Child Jesus—under her gracious and smiling appearance—is in reality a soul of combat.

"You will make no progress unless you do violence to yourself"[9] was not dead for Therese. During her last illness, she said to one sister, "I make many little sacrifices."

These lines, her own, sum up her sainthood.

> Smiling, I face the fray,
> O my Spouse Divine;
> Singing, I go down fighting
> In that embrace of Thine.

Practical Application

"I want to become a saint," confided Celine Martin to the servant of God, "but, tell me, am I being too bold?"

"By no means," answered Therese, "even our Lord said: 'Be perfect as your heavenly Father is perfect!' He does not ask us to imitate the greatest saints, but He gives us the infinite holiness of His Father as the sum total of our ideal, and He commands us to be like Him."

It is clear, then, we are duty-bound to sanctify ourselves. But can we? By our own strength, no. With the supernatural help of grace, yes.

God cannot expect the impossible. He makes it possible for us to live up to the superhuman effort which he asks of us.

Making up for our weakness, He becomes our divine collaborator in this difficult task. "I can do all things in Him Who strengthens me,"[10] the apostle affirmed after declaring his own weakness.

We will prove that sanctity—in the measure of our predestination, of course—is unquestionably in the heart. And we have the power and the duty to acquire it.

Why, then, is there so little sanctity, even among those dedicated to it?

"It is because they do not will it," we learn from St. Bernard. Or if they do will it, they are so feeble that even the devil could not care less. St. Therese of the Child Jesus was not this way.

"I wish to become a saint," Therese said. And she did. But to do this she had to break her will, to swallow her pride, to change her character, to chastise her body, to mortify her heart. "Nothing is too much to win the palm!" she said. That is what is meant by willing to become a saint.

This proud woman who 'refused to kiss the ground', accepted an unjust accusation in silence.

This stubborn young girl, who preferred 'to sleep in the cellar' rather than yield to another, obeyed at the first word.

This little conqueror divested herself of all things without complaint.

Are we going to be less courageous than a four-year-old? Does not our cowardice make us blush? Let us start today to conquer ourselves.

Which of our hundred-and-one faults will we seize first? The most prominent, of course. We determine what measures to take to eliminate it. We anchor our resolutions with prayer. We foresee the occasions for struggle.

Are we overcome? Never be discouraged. Let us say with the simplicity of our saint. "It does not matter if I fall at each moment. I thereby feel my weakness, and I derive great profit from it. My God, You see what I am if You do not sustain me in Your arms."

COLLOQUY: With St. Therese of the Child Jesus.

I understand that in order to become a saint, one must suffer much, choose always what is most perfect, and forget oneself.

St. Therese of the Child Jesus

Notes

1. Letter of May 5, 1873.
2. Letter of May 22, 1873.
3. Note of Sr. Marie of the Sacred Heart.
4. Letter of December 5, 1875.
5. From one of Madame Martin's letters.
6. Letter dated May 14, 1896.
7. R. P. Carbonel, S. J., *Biography of St. Therese of the Child Jesus.*
8. Judith 15: 2.
9. *Imitation of Christ,* Book I, Ch. 25, 2.
10. Philip 4:13.

Chapter Two
Her Faith

My heaven is to smile at the God Whom I adore
When He hides Himself from me to prove my faith,
To smile until it pleases Him to recognize me again.
This is heaven for me!

St. Therese of the Child Jesus

The vitality of her faith is clear in *The Story of a Soul*. This theological virtue, planted by baptism in all Christian souls, was simply increased in the heart of this predestined child.

"She was determined," say those who knew her intimately, "not to stain her white baptismal robe, and to be faithful to the promises made by her godmother in her name at the baptismal font."[1]

The spiritual household, into which providence had placed her, contributed much to the development of a special mental outlook in this saint.

She was prematurely animated by the "spirit of faith" which should not be confused with the "theological virtue of faith." The latter, however, is regarded as a supernatural tendency which stems from the former.

She saw God in his works. And from the age of three, this imitator of Moses on Mt. Sinai adored the Lord.

11

Lightening, thunder, filled her with admiration instead of alarm.

"I feared nothing at all," she said. "I felt the goodness of God all around me. I was enraptured."

There was the same spirit of faith when she first saw the ocean.

"Its majesty," she said, "the roaring of the waves, all spoke to my soul of the omnipotence of God."

And lastly, during her pilgrimage to Switzerland, the beauty of creation lifted her to the Creator. "Towards the One," she wrote, "Who is pleased to fling such masterpieces on a land of exile which can last but only a day."

But in a soul so poised as hers, her conclusions were always practical. She said, "Later, when a prisoner of Carmel and I can see no more than a tiny corner of the sky, the remembrance of these delightful things will give me courage. I will not make much of the little things that concern me but think rather of the greatness of God; I will love Him in a special way, and will not be so unfortunate as to attach myself to 'straws,' now that my heart has had a glimpse of what is reserved for those who love Him."

And so, if—in the presence of the material works of God—the faith of Therese is so rooted, what can be said of her dispositions to the liturgical ceremonies?

"The feasts! What soothing memories this simple word reminds me of," exclaimed this chosen soul. "My little mother explained so well to me the mysteries hidden in each of them. These particular days became for me heavenly days!"

Therese called Sunday "God's feast day," the day she liked best.

"Her respect for holy things was edifying," those who knew her tell us. "It bore witness to her sincere belief in the power which is attached to blessed objects."

In her naive faith, the little queen found a special flavor in blessed bread. She would meticulously examine her rosary beads after the priest blessed them. She had to see what blessed beads looked like?

"Light the blessed candle," she said during her last illness in the infirmary. "Its presence consoles me; I feel that it puts the devil to flight."

But sacraments, even more than the sacramentals, attracted this soul of faith.

"My little Therese," Pauline had said to her before her first confession, "it is not a man, but God himself to whom you will tell your sins."

The Benjamin answered with the faith of a saint, the logic of a child, letting out awkward facts. "Then, dear mother, might I not tell the Reverend Ducellier that I love him with all my heart?"

Receiving her first absolution, she recalled, "At that moment, the tears of the little Jesus purified my soul."

From then on, she confessed often, "because confession filled her whole being with joy."

At her first Communion, she was like an angel. Her sister Celine said of this, "Therese was confirmed on June 14, 1884. The four days which preceded it are particularly memorable ones for me. 'My little sister who was usually so calm was not the same. A sort of holy enthusiasm took hold of her. As I showed my astonishment in this matter, she explained to me how the Holy Spirit would take possession of her soul at Confirmation. Her language was so inspiring, and she looked so earnest that I was filled with a supernatural awe and parted from her deeply moved.'"[2]

Her whole life of prayer and holy contemplation was based on faith.

"What pleases me when I call to mind the interior life of the Holy Family," she confided, "is to think that they led a very ordinary life. The Holy Virgin and St. Joseph knew well that Jesus was God, but the marvelous thing about it is that they remained hidden and like us, 'they lived by faith.'"

The luminous and intelligent character of her faith

While doubt is not diabolical in itself, it is almost always a form of ignorance—dogmatic ignorance, that is. One can be a great scholar, yet be ignorant of the ABCs of the catechism and apologetics—even more so of theology.

Objections, irrefutable to nonbelievers, would collapse like cardboard houses if only they made them known to a priest.

Doubters are usually ill-informed. But pious knowledge in believers can sometimes be detrimental, too.

Implicit faith is certainly praiseworthy, but that of a theologian is preferable. Therese understood this. For her, theological virtue was never synonymous with agnorance. From her earliest years, she set to strengthen her faith through study of the catechism. She especially liked the lives of the saints and church history.[3]

During religious instruction she answered, with rare precision, the questions asked by the Reverend Domin, chaplain of the boarding school. Therese was so acute, the priest nicknamed her his "little doctor." She was especially intuitive about heaven and things beyond the grave.

Conferences of the Reverend Arminjon on the end of the world and the mysteries of the life beyond particularly appealed to her, because they helped her mediate on mysteries unknown to her.

"The perusal of that work," she wrote, "plunged my soul into unearthly happiness; I already had a presentiment of what God reserves for those who love Him. Seeing how out of proportion are eternal rewards with the flimsy sacrifices of this life, I wanted to love Jesus passionately, to give Him a thousand marks of tenderness while I was still able."

This servant of God always remained orthodox. She was uncompromising regarding obedience due ecclesiastical authority.

She valued a certain book highly. Learning eventually that the author lacked respect for a bishop, she rejected his works and never again wanted to hear about them.[4]

During trial, she practiced the counsel of St. Peter to the first Christians. "Resistite fortes in fide."[5] Resist you, strong in faith. That was the secret of her invincible fortitude, the arsenal of her strong will.

Therese arrived at Carmel only after many difficulties. But the young aspirer showed courage. She applied to herself the divine words, "Why are you fearful? Are you still without faith?"[6]

"A person whose heart is always restless," she wrote, "shows that it needs miracles in order to strengthen it. Its faith is like a mustard seed; but as for Jesus' intimate friends, for His Mother, there was no need to work wonders to prove their faith. Did He not allow Lazarus to die, although Martha and Mary had fore-warned Jesus that he was ill? At the wedding feast at Cana, did He not answer the Holy Virgin that His hour had not yet come?"

But after the test, what a reward! Water was changed into wine, Lazarus was brought back to life. Jesus treated little Therese the same. After trying her for a long time, He fulfilled her desires.

But what did these desires consist of? Was she carried away by extraordinary graces, splendid achievements?

No, Therese's ambition was to bury herself behind the im-penetrable grilles of Carmel, becoming the spouse of Christ in faith. "Sponsabo te mihi in fide."[7]

She desired neither spiritual consolation, nor revelation. "I do not wish to see God here on earth," she said. "My little way is the practice of blind faith."

A novice told her how radiant angels would soon lead her into paradise. She replied, "All these imaginings do me no good." "God and the angels are pure spirits; no one can see them with the eyes of the body as they are in reality. I can only nourish myself on Truth."

No one can judge a soldier's worth until seeing him on the battlefield. The same goes for spiritual evaluation.

From youth, Therese wished to prove the transcendant reality of her faith by the sacrifice of her life.

Visiting the underground palace of the Doges in Venice, she was reminded of the bloody era of persecution.

"I would have chosen joyously to live in those frightful dungeons," she affirmed, "if it was a question of confessing my faith."

At Rome, in the arena of the ruins of the Colosseum, she knelt on the paved transept where the martyrs had once struggled. Kissing the ground with emotion, she asked heaven to grant her the same favor.

"In the depths of my heart, I felt that I was heard." she said.

And she admitted, "Underneath it all, I want to be a martyr. Martyrdom! that is the dream of my youth; this desire has increased within me in my little Carmelite cell."

This desire was realized, but not as the holy Carmelite wished. She did not show her faith by dying for it, but by living for eighteen months in the most painful anguish of spirit. A few days after her lung hemorrhage on Good Friday, 1896, God permitted St. Therese of the Child Jesus to be violently tempted until her death.

On tempted faith, M. Leopold Levaux, a Belgian critic, wrote, "One doubts what one does not see; but there is no doubt involved when one does not see what was never meant to be seen but known only by faith. . . .

"'Faith says well what the senses do not say,' writes Pascal, 'but not the opposite of what they see. It is above the senses and not contrary to them'; and again: 'Obedience and the use of reason constitute true Christianity.' Reason proves faith; then. . . ."

The temptation to doubt is horribly painful; but the faithful will does not surrender one iota. . . . When St. Therese of the Child Jesus no longer sees anything but darkness, it is the effect of divine intervention which procures her sanctification and attends to her merits: 'Although not experiencing the enjoyment of faith, I force myself to make acts of faith,' she says. . . . " 'My just man lives by faith.' (St. Paul). This is the way the heroism of Therese and the mercy of God are manifested to us. God gives us a resolute sister to whom we can cling in our own nights. It is very much the opposite of doubt. It is because of your saintliness, Oh, little sister, that having done what you had to do and having carried the burdens that you had to carry, that you have 007 imitation   13

"It seems to me," Therese said of her sufferings, "that in this darkness, evil voices speak mockingly: 'You dream of light, of a sweet-scented country, of the eternal possession of the Creator of all these wonders . . . you think that one day you will leave this fog where you languish . . . Dream on! dream on! . . . you rejoice in death which will give you, not what you hope for, but a night even more obscure, that of annihilation.' " The defensive attitude of Therese in this critical period reveals an extraordinary prudence. Knowing it unwise to argue with temptation, she took flight at each attack. Her flight, far from cowardly, resembled the wise tactics of the Horatii against the three Curatii.

"At each new occasion of combat," she said, "I conduct myself bravely: knowing that it is cowardice to fight a duel, I turn my back on my adversary and refuse to face him.

"Then I run towards Jesus and tell Him that I am ready to shed my blood in order to proclaim that there is a heaven; I tell Him that I am happy not to catch a glimpse down here of this paradise which awaits me so that He will open it for all eternity to poor unbelievers.

"O my God," she continued, "if it is necessary that the faith contaminated by them be purified by one soul who loves You, I desire very much to eat there the bread of tears alone. The special grace I ask of You, is never to offend You."

St. Therese of the Child Jesus not only kept her faith, she turned it into heroism.

With her own blood, Therese wrote the entire Credo on the

first page of the Gospels which she carried near her heart. Though she did not brag of it.

"I have made more acts of Faith in one year than all the rest of my life," she wrote in her autobiography before her death. It was not, however, without struggle.

One morning in August 1897, Mother Agnes of Jesus came into the infirmary and found her little sister in contemplation before the holy face.

"I have been awake all night," she confided. "I have successfully repelled temptations. Oh! I have made so many acts of faith."

Another time, Mother Agnes talked to her about heaven. St. Therese sighed.

"You are showing me how much you are suffering interiorly," Pauline said to her. Then adding, "How can a person love God and the Blessed Virgin so much and still have such thoughts as these?"

At first sight, it seems inconceivable that such a soul, geared toward the supernatural, could doubt the existence of heaven.

God permitted Therese to be enveloped in darkness, her sufferings separating her will from her understanding.

No consolation came to end her uncertainty that night. Only a few lights on her nothingness completed her mortification and detached her from herself.

Once when Mother Agnes of Jesus spoke to her about interior lights on heaven which the Holy Spirit sometimes accords to his spouses, Therese answered, "As far as I am concerned, I have only lights on my nothingness, but that does me more good than lights on faith."

She willingly sacrificed these supernatural lights for the profit of other souls guilty of voluntary blindness.

On September 2, she confided to her sister, "I have especially offered my interior trials for one of our relatives who does not have the faith."

Moreover, Therese rejoiced in her suffering—not only because it was a means of obtaining light for poor sinners, but more so because she wanted to give God all her love.

"It is so good to serve God in darkness and trial! We have only this life to live by faith," she told a novice, while on her deathbed. Also, she said, "If I had not been tried against faith, I believe I would die of joy at the thought of soon leaving this earth!"

Therese did not die of joy. Spouse of the divine, she breathed her last as Jesus did. "Was it not necessary for Him to suffer and so enter into His glory?"[9]

Rejoicing, she said, "What I have believed, I have seen; that which I have desired, I possess; I am united in heaven to the One Whom I have loved so singularly on earth."

Practical Application

To understand the value of faith, we should consider the esteem which Jesus Christ had for it.

Not content with establishing theological virtue as the condition *sine qua non* of our salvation, He has imposed it in a peremptory manner on those who would ask some miracle from him.

"Do you believe that I can heal you?" He asked. And if the answer was yes, He sent them away safe, saying, "Go, your faith has saved you."

Once, someone expressing her absolute faith in Him, he was moved, Words of admiration fell from His lips. "O woman, your faith is great!"

It would seem that the heroic saint of Lisieux merits this divine praise also.

To simple and sincere souls, the servant of God gives the idea of a lucid spirit of faith which finds divine meaning in all things. Even to souls who are tormented, to intellectuals with their cunning objections, she is a teacher.

"What a beautiful lesson of faith the virgin of Lisieux has given to us in her trials!" wrote Monsignor Baudrillart.

"Though a soul may be candid and have good will, in times like ours it is practically impossible that the man who studies and who thinks and who, because of the circumstances and the needs arising from his occupations, may not at some time or other be tempted in his faith.

"Well! God in His infinite wisdom has allowed Therese, in the midst of grievous illnesses, to know also that anguish of faith; and although living in the light of the supernatural, she experienced the unreality of this supernatural."[10]

May souls tempted like hers have recourse. She has known their anxiety; she has understood it; she has sympathized with it; she has responded victoriously by acts of faith against suggestions of doubt.

If these souls are fashioned as resistantly as a saint's, she will teach them to carry that cross while rejoicing, "Lord, all that you do fills me with joy!"[11]

"The less one's intense suffering appears to the eyes of men, the more it pleases you, O my God. And if, by some impossibility You, Yourself, became ignorant of it, I would still be happy to suffer in the hope that my tears would be able to prevent or to make up for one single fault against faith."

However violently we are tempted, let us not be troubled. Deprived of a sensible faith, let us sing nevertheless of what we want to believe. May our canticle of love, rising above the roaring of the waves, teach us through the divine helmsman that the faith of the little cabin boy is still alive.

And if, by some misfortune, we feel weighed down and faint-hearted, let us glance confidently toward the beacon who bestows on souls the brightness of true doctrine.

Let us believe unreservedly what the Church teaches, having faith in its supernatural and divine mission. And let us find in her, freedom for our soul, peace for our heart, and truth for our mind.

COLLOQUY: With the God of all goodness. Let us recite the Creed.

> In the shadow of faith, I love You
> The God of my heart I adore
> O Jesus, to see You I wait
> In peace on the morning shore.
>
> *St. Therese of the Child Jesus*

Notes

1. *The Spirit of St. Therese of the Child Jesus,* p. 66.
2. Testimony of Sr. Genevieve of the Holy Face at the process of the ordinary, p. 123.
3. Monsignor Laveille, *St. Therese of the Child Jesus,* p. 105.
4. *The Spirit of St. Therese of the Child Jesus,* p. 71.
5. I Peter 5:9.
6. Mark 4:40.
7. Osee 2:20.
8. *The Catholic Review of Ideas and Fads,* February 5, 1926.
9. Luke 24:26.
10. In the preface of the *Biography of St. Therese of the Child Jesus* by Msgr. Laveille.
11. Ps. 91:4.

Chapter Three
Her Hope

When I dream of immortal life
I no longer feel the burden of my exile
Soon I will take wing for the first time
O! my God! towards my only home.

St. Therese of the Child Jesus

"Mama," asked three-year-old Therese, "will I go to heaven?"

"Yes, if you are good."

"Then, if I were not good, mama, would I go to hell? But I know what I would do. I would fly away with you who will be going to heaven; then you would hold me tight in your arms. How would God catch me then?"

This blind confidence of little ones towards their mother, the orphan Therese transferred to God. With a pious assurance, she would affirm later, "Little children are not damned!"

Even though she was peacefully assured, her hope was still subject to severe trials.

Shortly after her first communion, persistent scruples tormented her. Her most innocent thoughts and simplest actions—like having tied sky-blue ribbons in her hair—as any child might do playfully—passed through the sieve of her fearful conscience.

She found some comfort in owning up to her transgressions.

But even this respite passed quickly, her martyrdom beginning. It lasted two years.

The departure of Marie for Carmel crowned the anxiety of the little Benjamin. No longer able to confide her torments to her elder sister, the little flower turned its petals heavenward.

She addressed the four little angels, her brothers and sisters, who had preceded her there.

"You have never known trouble and fear," she said to them. "Have pity on your poor little sister who is suffering here on earth."

Her adolescent scruples soon disappeared. Peace moved her soul and confirmed her forever with hope. The little innocents had carried her request to the Most High.

Taught by painful experience, the young saint later excelled in enlightening scrupulous souls.

"Since you are humble enough to ask advice of Therese," she wrote Marie Guerin, "she is going to tell you what she thinks.

"The devil knows that he cannot make a soul sin who wishes to be entirely surrendered to God; he tries only to persuade her that she has sinned. Even that is a lot; but for his fury it is not enough. Since he is not able to penetrate the soul, he at least wishes it to remain empty and without a master.

"Do not listen to the devil; make fun of him, and go to receive Jesus without fear in peace and in love."

"But I can hear you saying: 'That's what Therese thinks because she does not understand my distress. . . .' Yes, she does understand; she guesses all. She, too, has passed through the martyrdom of scruples, but our Lord has given her the grace to communicate often even though she feels she has committed great sins. It is the only way to shake off the tempter. If he sees that he is wasting his time, he leaves us in peace."[1]

Assuredly, Therese had weathered the storm of scruples without shipwreck. Yet there remained still two other stumbling blocks to her hope—despair and presumption. She handled these upon meeting them.

"The remembrance of my faults humiliates me," she wrote the Reverend Belliere, her spiritual brother. "It teaches me never to rely on my strength which is only weakness; but more so, this remembrance speaks to me of mercy and of love."

Can one reconcile confidence in God with mistrust of self?

"Discouragement did not take hold of her," her biographer tells us.[2] "She felt her weakness; her terrible interior arridities were a threat to her strength; and yet she was only more vigilant in the practice of her duties."

This is confirmed by Therese. "Whenever I commit a small fault," she confided, "I am never discouraged. On the contrary, I abandon myself into the arms of Jesus. I bury myself deeper, like a little dewdrop, into the chalice of the divine Flower of the Field, and there I find again all that I have lost and still more."

By what artifice did this little dewdrop so regally claim her treasures?

"I recount in detail to God all my infidelities," she explained. "I expect, in my reckless abandon, to acquire an even greater command over His Heart, and to draw more fully to myself the love of Him 'Who did not come to call the just but sinners.'"[3]

The servant of God was not governed by fear, rather by an apostle of love.

"My way is all confidence in God," she affirmed. "I do not understand souls who fear such a loving Friend."

After reading "He gives to each one according to his works,"[4] a novice asked Therese, "Why does it say 'according to his works' since St. Paul speaks of being justified by the free gift of his grace?"[5]

These texts, appearing contradictory, did not disturb the young theologian. She answered, "We must act as if all depended on us, and hope as if all depended on God."

A fearful soul once handed St. Therese of the Child Jesus this objection. "God finds blemishes even in His angels; how can you really expect me not to tremble at the thought of judgment?"

She answered, "It is only a way of prevailing upon God not to judge us at all; it is to reserve nothing for oneself, to apply all its merits to souls."

"But if God does not judge our good actions, then will He not judge our bad ones?"

"What are you saying? Our Lord is justice itself. If He does not judge the good, He will not judge the bad." And continuing, "For victims of love, it seems to me that there will be no judgment; but rather God will hasten to reward, by eternal happiness, His own Love which He will see burning in their heart."

St. Therese built her audacious hope on this thought. "The fire of love is more purifying than the fire of justice," this replacing purgatory.

But the prospect of a stay in that place of exile did not frighten her. Her trust knew no bounds.

"If you knew how sweet my judgment will be!" she exclaimed, "and if God should chide me even a tiny bit, I will still find it sweet. If I do go to purgatory, I will still be happy. I will act like the three Hebrews and walk in the furnace singing the Canticle of Love."

An intuition told her that she would attain an eminent degree of sanctity.

"I always feel the same bold confidence of becoming a great saint," she wrote her prioress. "I do not count on my own merits, since I don't have any, but I hope in Him Who is virtue and sanctity itself. He alone Who is contented with my feeble efforts will raise me up to Himself and make me a saint."

These dreams of glory and heavenly blessedness, legitimate as they were, nevertheless did not constitute the essential object of her hope.

She clung tenaciously to this divine promise, "I, Myself, will be your great reward."[6]

One summer evening during her last illness the infirmary window was open, a distant melody playing.

Now, Therese enjoyed music. Though during her confinement to Carmel, where the recto tono chant is obligatory in choir, she was deprived these melodies. But she said, "Soon in Heaven I will hear wonderful harmonies. . . ." But her thought, after revelling a moment in this enchanting prospect, turned itself toward God.

She confided to her little mother, "Only one hope beats in my heart: the love which I have received and which I will give. Oh! to love, to be loved, and to come back to earth to make Love loved!"

These statements prove that the angelic nun of Lisieux did not hope in vain.

It seems that God almost wishes by these examples to give us this lesson. "Learn that I am niggardly towards those who fear Me, and that I overwhelm with generosity the humble and the little who hope in me. Therese, my beloved daughter, repeats to all who will hear her, 'One can never have too much confidence in God; one obtains all that one hopes for from him.' The shower of roses she scattered on earth proves to you how magnificently I treat souls who honor me by never doubting."

The fervent Carmelite already received the pledge of divine splendor in the infirmary of Carmel where she put the finishing touches to her sanctification.

"It is incredible," she confided, "how all my hopes are realized! When I read St. John of the Cross, I begged God to effect in me what was described there; namely, to sanctify me in a few years as much as if I had lived to old age. In a word, to consume me rapidly in love . . . and I was heard!"

Exercising her duties, Therese often repeated, "Confidence can do all things; it obtains miracles." She desired to find this untarnished virtue in the hearts of her novices.

One of them told her of the strong opposition there was in the community to admit her to profession. When all seemed hopeless, St. Therese of the Child Jesus asked her, "Are you confident of good results just the same?"

"Yes, I am convinced that I will obtain that grace and nothing can make me doubt it." Firmly, Therese answered, "Keep your confidence. It is impossible that God will not answer you because He always measures His gifts to our hope. However, I confess that if I had seen you hesitate, I myself would doubt since, humanly speaking, all hope is lost."

The novice was admitted and became a fervent religious.[7]

If the saint demanded that her daughters place their confidence in God, even in the most trying situations, she was the first to give them a courageous example of it.

When she was hurt by the long illness of M. Martin, not once did her hope waver.

"At the time of our great trial when it was my turn to be versicularian in choir, you will never know with what sentiment of abandonment I pronounced the lofty versicle: 'In Te Domine, speravi.'"[8]

Although she was convinced that the will of God was best, she still did not wish to oppose any formal demand.

"On my Profession Day, Mother Mary of Gonzaga constrained me to beg for the recovery of our dear father, but I could make no other prayer than this one: 'My God, I beseech You, let Papa recover if it is *Your* Will!'"

Apparently, it was not God's Will because not only did M. Martin not get better, but Therese herself suffered a mortal illness a few years later.

The Lord, having resolved to make his spouse a masterpiece of hope, perfected her virtue by painful trials. Sickness racked her body while doubt clutched her soul. The courageous Carmelite magnanimously accepted these misfortunes with serene joy.

On Good Friday 1896, seeing her handkerchief stained with blood, she cried out with joy, "Oh!, Mother, what hope! I thought I had learned good news. The hope of going to heaven transports me with joy!"

This hope, as we have seen, underwent cruel combat by the spirit of darkness. Under his occult influence, Paradise—which seemed so real to Therese and for which she had an intense longing—was presented to her as an illusion, like a shadow blurred on the horizon.

She had the false impression that beyond death the abyss of nothingness awaited her. The ideal of her life seemed to her nothing more than a deceptive myth. She felt condemned.

But her confidence in God never wavered. The evil one attacked her faith and hope at once, but gratitude still flowed from her pen.

"Never have I been so aware that the Lord is sweet and merciful. He has sent this heavy cross to me only at the moment when I am able to bear it. I believe it would discourage me at another time; now it produces only one thing: to quicken all natural satisfaction in my longing for Heaven."

Her soul in darkness, her body on the cross, Therese remained for eighteen months resplendent.

God tried her as his servant of old, Job. The same cry of love escaped from her lips. "Let Him kill me if He will; I have no other hope."[9]

"The word of scripture is not impressed on my heart in vain," said the saint. "I confess that I was a long time coming to this degree of hope; now that I am here, it is the Lord's doing."
Adding, "If a soul is disheartened, if she sometimes despairs, it is because she is thinking of the past and the future. In the meantime, pray for me; often when I storm heaven to come to my aid, it is then that I am most desolate."

"How is it that these desolations do not discourage you?" Therese was asked.

"I turn to God, to all the saints, and I even thank them; I believe that they want to see how far my hope can be pushed!"

One day when she was particularly tried Mother Agnes of Jesus said to her, "You are suffering so much! Are you discouraged or sad?"

"Oh! no! I am not at all unhappy . . . God gives me just what I am able to bear."

She was not troubled at the prospect of further martyrdom.

"I do not fear the worst struggles nor the greatest sufferings. God always comes to my aid; He has led me by the hand since my childhood; I count on Him. Suffering will reach extreme limits, but I am sure that He will never abandon me."

She did not flinch from the tide of suffering surging toward her, ready to engulf her. She courageously rose above the distress of her abandoned and tempted soul.

"What's going to become of me?" she wrote. "To die of sorrow at seeing myself so helpless? Oh! no, I am not even going to be troubled by it.

"With delightful surrender, I wish to fix my gaze on the Divine Sun until death. Nothing will be able to frighten me....

"If dark clouds should come to hide the star of love, this would be the moment of pushing my confidence to its utmost limits, knowing that beyond the dismal clouds my sweet sun still shines."

Practical Application

The heroic stand of the Carmelite nun of Lisieux is a model for all those who suffer.

Since we will all suffer sometime, let us learn like St. Therese to draw profit from our trials and look at them supernaturally.

From this view we will find occasions (1) to expiate our sins; (2) to sanctify ourselves; (3) to save our souls; (4) to glorify God. These are unquestionable spiritual advantages, weights counterbalancing the bitterness experienced by nature.

Whatever our crosses, we will never be discouraged. On the contrary, let us rejoice with the apostles "to have had the honor of suffering humiliation for the sake of Christ."[10]

Let us follow the example of St. Therese to fear God less as judge, love him more as father.

Perhaps someone will object, "Why is it surprising that St. Therese of the Child Jesus excelled in hope? Did she not have, perfect as she was, everything to hope for and nothing to fear from divine justice?"

Yes, she did. But she did not base her confidence on perfection but on the mercy of the Lord.

"It is not because I have been preserved from mortal sin that I have confidence in God," she wrote. "Even if I would have on my conscience all the crimes which can be committed I would lose nothing of my conviction. I would repent and throw myself into the arms of my Savior. I know that He loves dearly the prodigal child, I have heard His words to Magdalen, to the woman taken in adultery, to the Samaritan. I know what draws me to His love and His mercy."

And again, "Oh, Jesus! I would like to tell all little souls of your ineffable condescension! I feel that if, by some impossibility, You would find a soul weaker than mine You would be pleased to load it with even greater favors, provided that it abandon itself with full confidence to Your infinite mercy."

The way is marked. Let us practice what St. Therese of the Child Jesus taught.

COLLOQUY: With Our Lord.

> I know well that I will never be worthy of what I hope for; but I hold you by the hand like a little beggar, and I am sure that You will hear me fully because You are so good.[11]
>
> *St. Therese of the Child Jesus*

Notes

1. Her cousin, the future Marie of the Eucharist.
2. *St. Therese of the Child Jesus*, Monsignor Laveille, p. 241.

3. Matt. 9:13.
4. Sir. 16:14.
5. Rom. 3:24.
6. Gen. 15:1.
7. *St. Therese of the Child Jesus*, Monsignor Laveille, pp. 342–343.
8. Ps. 21:1, "In Thee, O, Lord, have I hoped."
9. Job 13:15.
10. Acts 5:41.
11. *Summarium of 1919*, pp. 594–595.

Chapter Four
Her Love for God

It is of the greatest importance that the soul
exercises itself much in love so that being rapidly consumed, it will not tarry here below
but come promptly to see its God face to face.

St. John of the Cross

"Certain directors counsel their penitents to count their acts of virtue," wrote the servant of God to Celine, "but my Director Who is Jesus teaches me to do everything for love."

Therese was, without suspecting it perhaps, of the school of St. Francis de Sales to whom someone said, "I wish to acquire charity through humility... humility through charity."

There would have to be many pages devoted to the complete study of this theological virtue which was, in the soul of this angelic nun, like a well which the other virtues came to draw.

Her active and dedicated charity

St. Therese was not of those superficial souls whose love of God consists mainly in declarations to which their actions correspond little. On the contrary, she proved her tenderness by devotion which never contradicted itself.

There are two ways of doing this: to work for the glory of the one who is loved, or simply to please him.

Therese worked at each of these effectively, but wrongly

33

judged herself unfit to serve God and thought she could in any event amuse him and make him happy. This was her main objective. And there is every reason to believe that she has accomplished it.

"Great saints have worked for the glory of God," she said, "but since I am only a little soul, I spend myself for His pleasure alone.

"I wish to be a little flower in the hand of God, an unpetaled rose, but one whose appearance and fragrance may still be something like a diversion to Him; even His joy."

What did she do to become "God's little joy"?

The first thing she did was receive with a smile whatever God sent. Then she worked for Him with the fervor of a diligent bee "not allowing any little sacrifice, any look, any word to escape her—profiting by the smallest actions, and doing them for love."

When she found herself in dryness, she did not seek relaxation, but forced herself to rekindle the fire smoldering under the ashes, throwing twigs on it, "mere nothings which please Jesus."

Many years ago, a French prelate said frankly, "I love Therese because she does not work with God on a mathematical basis."

"Consume my whole being," she would be able to say like her little sister of Dijon.[1] "Go on, do not stand upon ceremony, am I not sincerely Yours?"

"Ah! let us give, let us give to Jesus," she recommended to Celine. "Let us be lavish with Him."

And to a novice who was fond of herself she said, "You withdrew then from the world in order to seek rest? As for me, I came here in order to give more to God. Recall that fitting sentence of *The Imitation*: 'As soon as one begins to seek herself, at that moment she ceases to love....'"

As for Therese, her comforts, her reputation, even her own satisfaction, were not taken into account. She soared above these trifles of self-love.

"There is only one thing to do here below," she declared, "that is to love Jesus with all the strength of our heart and to save souls for Him."

In order that the little queen would have something to look forward to in paradise, God inspired her with the knowledge that she would still be able to save souls after death.

But something still bothered this heroic virgin, something which not even God would have wanted to remedy.

"Alas," she told herself, "I would no longer take into account the price of love. I would offer myself up in joy and no longer in suffering."

She resolved to give all her tenderness by imposing on herself every possible hardship while she labored.

"At my death," she said, "when I shall see the good and ever-so-kind God Who will want to fill me with happiness for all eternity—and since I will no longer be able to prove my love by sacrifices—it will be impossible for me to bear up if I have not done all that I could have done on earth to give Him pleasure."

Her unselfish charity

The dedication of St. Therese of the Child Jesus was on an equal footing with absolute selflessness. During the retreat before profession, Christ provided her with the occasion of giving proofs of it.

"Your little daughter does not drink 'the sweet wine of the vineyards of Engaddi'[2] at all," she confided to Mother Agnes of Jesus. "Her nuptual journey is very dry."

The divine bridegroom made her walk in an obscure, dim underground passage. He held her hand, true, but without speaking.

Many in her place would have become vexed. But Therese was charmed.

"I am very happy not to have consolation," she said. "I would be ashamed if my love resembled that of earthly brides who look at the hands of their future spouses in order to see if they are holding some gift for them, or at their faces to catch a loving smile which enraptures them.... Therese, the little bride of Jesus loves Jesus for Himself." Adding, "I do not desire sensible love; provided Jesus is aware of it, that's enough for me."

Does this mean the saint was indifferent to the apparent coldness of her beloved? That would be wrong knowing her loving heart.

"It is a martyrdom to love Jesus without experiencing the sweetness of His love," she wrote Celine. "Very well! let us die martyrs.

"Oh! my little sister, let us detach ourselves from earth; let us fly towards the mountain of love where we will find delightful freedom for our souls. Let us detach ourselves from consolations of our Lord in order to attach ourselves to Him alone."

The angelic nun was distressed by the sudden change in the apostles—so enthusiastic on Sunday, so unreliable on Friday.

"Who, then, wants to serve Jesus for Himself," she wrote. "Ah! I will be the one!"

Yes, little Therese, you are the one. You loved Jesus purely for himself.

"If, by some impossibility, God did not see my good actions, I would not be troubled by it. I love Him so much that I would want to please Him without His knowing it is I. Knowing it and seeing it He is almost bound to reward it and I do not want to put Him to that trouble!"

"What will you say if the joys of Heaven are found to be less than you had hoped for?" someone once asked her.

"That does not matter," she answered. "Anything that makes God happy is entirely sufficient for my happiness."

This, then, is willing-to-please love in its most selfless expression.

Her ardent love

Therese's love was tender, burning, equal to the most passionate lovers of the Crucified.[3]

"I want to love Him as He has never before been loved!" she

stammered. And "Oh my God, Your love has gone before me from my childhood; it has grown with me and now it is an abyss, the depths of which I cannot fathom."

"She loves God as a child loves its father with incredible tenderness."[4]

Her novices affirmed this. "She had tears in her eyes when she commented on the maxims of St. John of the Cross like this one: 'In the evening of life you will be judged on love. Learn then to love God as He ought to be loved and abandon yourself.'"

They did not think this emotion sentimental, short-lived enthusiasm. No, it was from a soul overflowing with love.

For Therese, all which could not nourish her love was considered nothing.

One day, Therese meditating in the garden, Mother Agnes of Jesus joined her. Therese confided, "How well I understand the word of our Lord to our Mother, St. Theresa: 'Do you know, my daughter, who those are who truly love Me? They are those who know that all which does not have reference to Me is only vanity."

With conviction, the servant of God attached herself to the one thing necessary for her existence: to love God with her heart, soul, strength, mind.

From divine love she had found the secret of reaping the harvest of her short existence.

"Love can supply for a long life. Jesus does not look at time since He is eternal; He pays attention only to love," she affirmed.

Always logical, the saint made her life a perpetual exercise in divine charity.

One day her sister Marie asked, "How is it that you are always thinking of God?"

"It is not difficult: one naturally thinks of those whom she loves," answered Therese.

"Then, do you ever lose sight of His presence?"

"Oh, no! I don't believe that I have ever been three minutes without thinking of Him."[5]

This union with God did not occur without special grace. In fact, on June 9, 1895, St. Therese of the Child Jesus offered herself as a sacrifice to merciful love. Heaven acknowledged this with a sign.

Just as Therese was pierced by a dart of the seraphim, she was enveloped by a celestial fire.

Shortly before her death, Mother Agnes of Jesus asking for an explanation of this signal, she answered, "My little Mother, I told you about this the same day it happened but you paid no attention to it." Indeed, Mother Agnes, then prioress, saw the event unimportant. So Therese never alluded to it again.

Obediently, Therese told her superior about the favors given her, but she did not flaunt them.

Asked again about the incident, she explained, "A few days after my offering to Merciful Love, I began to make the Way of the Cross when all of a sudden I felt myself wounded by a dart of fire so intense that I thought I would die. I do not know how to explain it; it is as if an invisible hand had plunged my whole being into the fire. Oh! what burning and what sweetness! I was consumed with love, and I felt that I would not be able to endure this ardor one minute, one second more without dying.

"I then understood what the saints say about these states which they experience so often. As for me, I have gone through it only once and for a single instant, then I soon fell back into my customary dryness."

This grace produced lasting effects. From then on, St. Therese of the Child Jesus seemed possessed by the Holy Spirit even more than before.

Possibly a secret Pentecost embraced her like the apostles in the Cenacle, giving her love divine breadth. Since love wishes to communicate itself, her ardor from then became so vehement that she subjected herself to the most delightful—yet cruelest, of martyrdoms.

Appeasingly, the Holy Spirit told her, "You are now in fetters, but later it will be the time of your conquests."

But divine love suffers no delay. Therese then consulted the mystics wounded by love.

First, she asked her mother, St. Theresa of Avila, whom love had made poetic. The mother replied, "I am dying because I do not die."

Death was not far from the little consumptive of Lisieux, yet this answer did not satisfy her. She wanted immediate results.

Quenched in heavenly cellars, intoxicated with love, knowing nothing, incapable of finding the company he pursued before, St. John of the Cross spoke to her of mystical rapture. "I no longer have any other duty," he told her, "since henceforth my whole work is to love."

Therese, declaring herself incapable of following this eagle into the staggering heights of the mystic, listened to this word of love.

"The least movement of pure love is worth more to the Church than all other works put together," her spiritual father said.

Little Therese, meditating deeply, looked for confirmation of this in Scripture. She turned to Epistles, her soul communicating with St. Paul, the sublime, passionate lover of Christ.

"You are looking for the most perfect gifts," said the apostle, "but I am going to show you a yet more excellent way."

"Which one?" Therese asked herself. She kept inquiring, ending by discovering that St. Paul, like her, considered charity above all else, "because it includes and surpasses every kind of apostolate."

"At last I had found rest!" she confided, "because the apostle explained how all the most perfect gifts are nothing without love; he pointed out that charity is the most excellent way to go safely to God....

"Consider the Mystical Body of Holy Church. I did not recognize myself in any of the members described by St. Paul; or rather, I wanted to recognize myself in all of them.

"Charity will give me the key to my vocation.

"I understood that, if the Church was a body composed of different members, the most necessary and the most noble of all the organs was not lacking to it; I understood that it had a heart, and that this heart was burning with love; I understood that love alone activated its members and that if love died out, apostles would no longer proclaim the gospel, martyrs would refuse to shed their blood.

"I understood that love included all vocations, that love was everything, that it embraced all times and all places because it is eternal!"

At this unexpected discovery, this child cried out the 'eureka' of Archimedes.

"I have found my place in the bosom of the Church," she wrote, "and it is Jesus Himself Who has given it to me. In the heart of the Church, my Mother, I will be love!

"Brilliant works are forbidden me; I can neither preach the gospel nor shed my blood. What does it matter? My brothers work in my stead and I, little child that I am, stay very close to the royal throne. I love for those who are struggling!"

But how will she witness her love, since love is proved by deeds?

"The little child will scatter flowers," she said simply. "It will send its perfume heavenwards; it will sing in a ringing voice the Canticle of Love."

But what purpose will these flowers and their songs serve?

"Ah! I know it well," she answered, "this scented downpour, these delicate and worthless petals, these love songs and such a little heart will charm You just the same, O my God.

"Yes, these nothings will give You pleasure; they will make smile the Church Triumphant who, wanting to play with its little child, will gather these unpetaled roses and let them pass through your Divine Hands in order to clothe them with infinite value; it will cast them upon the Church Suffering in order to comfort it, and on the Church Militant to bring it victory."

Always the fervent little Saint, giving herself up to these dreams of love, kept sight of her weakness.

"How can a soul so imperfect as mine aspire to the fullness of love?" she asked herself. "What, then, is this mystery? Why do you not reserve, O my singular Friend, these boundless yearnings for great souls, for the eagles who soar to the heights?

"Alas, I am just a poor little bird covered only with down; I am not an eagle, I simply have the eyes and the heart of one."

This angelic nun found her reason for existing: to love. But she declared her heart too small to unite with the Church.

Necessarily, Christ came to her aid, gave her his love, humbled himself before her nothingness, transformed her into himself.

"The law of fear has given place to the law of love," explained St. Therese. "That is why love has chosen me, a weak and imperfect creature, for a holocaust. Is this choice not worthy of love? Yes, in order that love may be fully satisfied it is necessary to humble itself to nothingness, and transform this nothingness into fire."

In the last pages of her autobiography she wrote, "O Word, O my Savior, You are the Eagle Whom I love and Who attracts me; it is You, Who darting forth toward the land of exile, have wished to suffer and to die in order to carry away all souls and plunge them into the very center of the Holy Trinity, eternal furnace of love! You are the one Who, rising again towards the inaccessible light, remains hidden in our vale of tears under the appearance of a white wafer in order to nourish me with Your own substance.

"Oh Jesus! let me tell You that Your love reaches to distraction . . . how is it that in face of this folly my heart does not rush towards You? How could my confidence have limits?

"Ah! for You, indeed, the saints too have behaved foolishly; they have done great things since they were eagles! As for me, I am too little to do big things, and my folly is to count on the angels and saints in order to fly up to You with Your own wings of love, O my Divine Eagle! For as long as You wish, I will keep my eyes fixed upon You; I want to be fascinated by Your heavenly glance, I want to become the prey of Your love.

"I live in the hope that one day You will gather me up and carry me off to the furnace of love in order to make me become forever Your happy victim."

Practical Application

Since we are Therese's imitators, why do we not imitate her action which worked so positively for her?

His Holiness Pius XI encourages us, saying, "Let us take as our own that prayer of St. Therese of the Child Jesus which closes the precious book of her life: 'O Jesus, we beg You to cast Your heavenly glance upon a great number of little souls and to choose from this world a legion of little victims worthy of Your love!' "[6]

Why do we not respond to the call of the Pope? Why do we not enroll under the banner of love?

We would not find in it an increase of suffering, since the oblation to divine mercy does not necessarily bring special trials as does justice.

However, we note its privileges as R.P. Martin defined it.

"The essential advantage of the offering is to make the soul live in an act of perfect love," he said, "that is to say, in the most sanctifying state which exists."[7]

But in order to persevere, words are not enough, Therese teaches us, "It is necessary to surrender oneself truly and totally, because one is consumed by love only in proportion as one surrenders herself to it."

The secondary advantages are: (a) to purify the soul of faults and frailty; (b) to crown a life of love by a death of love; (c) to lessen the rigor of judgment because "The fire of love is more purifying than that of justice." However, this is a question of faithful souls having lived in the perfection conducive to divine love; (d) Theology teaches that the degree of glory in heaven corresponds to the degree of charity here.

The act of oblation is therefore the divine lift, the little shortcut, which will lead us—provided we persevere—to a glorious destiny.

If grace invites us, let us make use of this way.

COLLOQUY: Oblation to merciful love reads,

"So that my life may be one act of perfect love, I offer myself as a Victim of Holocaust to Your Merciful Love, begging you to consume me without ceasing, allowing the waves of infinite tenderness which are shut up within You to overflow into my soul so that I may become a martyr of divine love, O my God!

"May this martyrdom, after having prepared me to appear before You, finally cause me to die, and may my soul take its flight without delay into the eternal embrace of Your Merciful Love!

"I desire, O my well-Beloved, with each beat of my heart, to renew this offering an infinite number of times until, the shadows having vanished, I can tell you again of my love, face to face, eternally!"[8]

COLLOQUY: Spiritual Bouquet

Consider St. Therese of the Child Jesus, true flower of love, coming from heaven to earth in order to astonish heaven and earth. Here is a heart, a tender childlike soul, which is at the same time apostolic to the point of heroism. She is filled up, vibrating with the love of God and the love of Jesus, with a tender and strong, simple and profound love, which inspires in her transports of filial abandon and the heroic achievements of the apostle and the martyr.

(Discourse of His Holiness Pope Pius XI, at the promulgation of the decree "Di Tuto," March 19, 1925)

Notes

1. Sr. Elizabeth of the Trinity.
2. Cant. 1:13.
3. *St. Therese of the Child Jesus*, Monsignor Laveille, p. 253.
4. *Summarium of 1919*, Deposition of Sr. Genevieve of the Holy Face.
5. *Summarium of 1919*, Deposition of Sr. Marie of the Sacred Heart, p. 577.
6. Pontifical homily in the Mass of the canonization, May 17, 1925.
7. *In La Petite Voie d'Enfance Spirituelle*, pp. 81–84.
8. Indulgence attached during life for the recitation of the act of oblation composed by St. Therese of the Child Jesus: (a) A partial indulgence of three hundred days each time the faithful recite the above offering, with a contrite heart and with devotion, at least from these words: "So that my life may be one act of perfect love." (b) A plenary indulgence each month under the usual conditions to all who will recite this act everyday for a month.
(Given at Rome, at the Sacred Penitentiary, July 31, 1923)

Chapter Five
Charity Towards Her Neighbor

To live of love is to sail on to the end
Scattering joy and peace in hearts,
Beloved Pilot! Charity urges me on
Because I see You in the souls of my Sisters.
St. Therese of the Child Jesus

During the summer of 1897—the last which she spent here below—St. Therese of the Child Jesus, seated in her wheelchair, wrote the last chapters of her autobiography.

The novices and one lay sister interrupted her writing.

Welcoming them, Therese said, "I am writing on fraternal charity. This is a case of practicing it. Oh! fraternal charity, it is everything on earth; one loves God in the measure that one practices it."

Her patient charity

"Ah! how good and how pleasant it is for brethren to dwell together in unity!"[1] With these joyful words, Carmelites receive their sisters when they take the habit.

This goodness, though unquestionable, is subject to change.

"My biggest penance is community life," declared St. Bernard.

Monsignor Laveille believed this statement could not be said better. "Different characters," he said, "differences in education, and the play on natural sympathies which one can subdue but

45

not entirely suppress are, for the most fervent religious, multiple and continuous occasions for practicing virtue.

"And what happens when this source of suffering is met with in those communities which are protected from the world; that is, in cloisters where a small number of persons—always the same ones—are constantly rubbing up, against each other?"[2]

Before giving an account of domestic discords, we must make sure we do not insinuate that there was no religious spirit in Therese's community.

Let us consider these extenuating circumstances:

(1) The petty annoyances mentioned in her autobiography appear excessive. When in reality they have been scattered over nine and a half years of religious life.

(2) The guilty ones were for the most part infirm, sick sisters. A few experiences will show how the state of health influences character. On the other hand, these religious were the first to acknowledge their faults.

(3) It is known that Therese was exceptionally sensitive to unpleasant behavior. But since it was permitted by God for her sanctification, she experienced much peace from it, as her autobiography explains.

"At last, the gates of Carmel closed behind me and I received the embraces of the loving Sisters who were as mothers to me, and a new family of whose devotion and tenderness the world does not know."

With these reservations, let us examine what Therese was exposed to.

Soon after entering the monastery, two religious began to annoy Therese each time they met her. The young postulant, distressed, wrote to her confidant, Mother Agnes of Jesus, "I am a poor little ball pierced all over with pinpricks. . . .

"It is true, the holes are very little but I suffer more from them than from a single big one. Oh! the little ball is trembling! . . . I am, nevertheless, very happy to suffer all that Jesus permits."

In choir, the novice was irritated for months by a sister who constantly figeted with her beads during prayer. This unnerved St. Therese of the Child Jesus, but for charity's sake she never showed emotion.

"I remained very quiet," she wrote, "but sometimes I was bathed in perspiration and all I could do was simply to make a prayer of suffering."

Meanwhile, through self-mastery, she succeeded "in loving this little disagreeable noise, and offering it with joy to Jesus as if it were the most delightful concert."

A similar cross befell her while working in the laundry where a clumsy companion splashed her continuously with dirty water.

A lover of cleanliness, Therese's first impulse was to draw back quickly, wiping her face. Changing her mind, she told herself, "How foolish would one be to refuse such treasures which were so generously offered to her."

Instead of being annoyed, she forced herself to desire this "so well that at the end of half an hour, I had really taken a liking to it."

These two examples prove it possible, despite protestations of nature, for one to willingly bring about a radical change in one's sentiments.

For several years, Therese's principal charge was assistant to an elderly religious whose trifling demands were as irritating as her slowness. It was a perpetual exercise of patience. One had to place her footstool in such a fashion, seat her in such a manner, and on and on.

With an amiability which might have led a person to think she had no internal struggle, St. Therese of the Child Jesus never let anyone notice her distress as she tried to keep peace.

This senior sister said later, "Oh! the dear little Sister! She was an angel; I could see it clearly." Adding, though everyone knew better, "I can also prove that I made her very happy."[3]

A novice, replacing the servant of God in helping the trying old sister, rebelled against her oddities, saying, "Never, Sister, did Sr. Therese of the Child Jesus speak to me as you have done!"

To the novice, Therese said of the remark, "Oh! be very kind to that poor Sister; she is ill. And, too, it is an act of charity, and at the same time an exercise in patience to let her think that she is interesting to us.

"We must be careful not to be provoked interiorly; we must calm our soul in advance by charitable thoughts. After that, patience becomes easy to practice."[4]

One day the servant of God nursed a sister with neurasthenia.

"Ah!" she cried, "how happy I would have been to be infirmarian in order to take care of that Sister! grace would have spoken louder than nature. Yes, I had a liking for all that . . . and I would have put all my love there! Oh! it seems to me that I would have made that Sister so happy, above all thinking of the words of Jesus: 'I was sick and you comforted Me.'"[5]

The most offending behavior, Therese favorably received it. As sacristan, the holy nun was abused one day. She was arranging flowers, sent from the outside, around the coffin of Reverend Mother Genevieve of St. Therese when a lay sister said to her peevishly, "It is easy to see that those wreathes were given by your family; the bouquets of the poor people are very well hidden!"

Therese answered affably, "Thank you, Sister, you are right. Give me the cross sent by the workmen; I will put it in front."[6]

A few years later, the remains of the little queen laid out in choir, this same sister kissed her feet, expressing contrition. At that moment she was cured of a cerebral anemia which had prevented her from reading and praying for a long time.

Exiled, Therese made use of suffering. She even looked for it. In one instance, she offered to assist a religious who had a contrary disposition. When Therese had just undergone bitter reproaches from her, a novice asked about the cause of her joyfulness.

"Sister x has just been saying disagreeable things to me," she answered. "Oh! how happy she has made me. I would like to meet her now with a smile."

At that moment this religious knocked at her door, and the novice was able to see how saints forgive.[7]

Charity not only moved her to support the irascibility of her neighbor, she even gracefully endured their lack of education, tact, and good taste.

During Therese's last stay in the infirmary, a sister in the community paid her a daily visit which, for anyone other than an extremely sick person, would have seemed humorous. Each evening she parted the bed curtains and mutely stared at Therese for a long while with a smile. Therese graciously returned her smiles. Mother Agnes of Jesus, seated at her bedside, thought this exchange must have either wearied or annoyed her sister.

Questioning Therese, she got the reply, "Yes, it is very painful to be looked at by someone who is laughing while one is suffering; but I think that on the cross our Lord had been very much looked at in the midst of his sufferings since the Gospel tells us that 'the passers-by jeered at Him; they shook their heads. . . . '[8] This thought enables me to offer Him this sacrifice good-naturedly."[9]

Another day, Mother Mary of Gonzaga asked her for a report of an oversight which would have been serious for her health. She confided to Mother Agnes of Jesus, "I had to tell our Mother the whole truth, but while speaking, there came to my mind a charitable expression of which I could avail myself and which was still not wrong; I followed my inspiration and God rewarded me for it by a deep interior peace."

Her tender and devoted charity

The gentle nun did not accept every affront with an angelic smile. No, this passive role was not enough for her charity. She had to give it free rein in sacrificing for her neighbor.

For the poor at Les Buissonets she made herself their advocate, doorkeeper, provider, comforter. Even the house servants experienced her kindness.

"Little Therese was very well brought up," wrote Victoire Pasquer, who had worked in the Martin home for seven years. "She won my admiration by her sweetness and her angelic expression. She was always as docile as a little angel...."

Her most altruistic thoughts were hidden behind the precocious face of a cherub. Later on, she said as much in these words.

"I felt so sorry for waitresses at great dinners. If by chance they happened to make some blunder, the lady of the house would look at them severely, and at this these poor people would blush with embarrassment and I said to myself: 'Ah! what a difference there is here below between masters and their servants—how well it proves that there is a heaven where each one will be ranked according to his interior worth, where everyone will be seated at the banquet of our Heavenly Father. But then, what a Servant will be ours! Since Jesus has said that He will go and come again to minister to us.'[10] This will be the moment for the poor and the little to be fully rewarded for their humiliations."

Already Therese demonstrated her affable nature at home. Upon entering Carmel, it grew even more.

If a postulant was upset, Mother Mary of Gonzaga would send her to Sr. Therese of the Child Jesus, knowing the novice was well-versed in consoling.

Once, encouraging a companion in the novitiate to conquer herself, Therese took on a routine compatible to that sister.

The obliging little novice took every opportunity to serve, no one suspecting. If a religious forgot her white mantle in the ante-choir, Sr. Therese of the Child Jesus quickly seized it, folded it, carefully put it back in place.

A feeble lay sister needed help back to the refectory each evening. Therese helped, even though the sister was unreasonably demanding.

Age and sickness had made this religious crochety. Despite Therese's care, the sister bellowed, "Ah! I said all along that you were too young to take care of me!"

Calmly, Therese continued her charitable service with ever so much love. She even cut the old sister's bread. Gradually the old sister took a liking to Therese.

Despite her frailities, St. Therese of the Child Jesus always took on the heaviest work. In the winter, the other sisters using warm water to do the laundry, she rinsed her linens in cold water. In the summer she did the reverse.

"In taking the most unpleasant tasks," she said, "one practices mortification towards oneself and charity towards others."

In 1891 an influenza epidemic hit the community. All but two got sick. Therese only suffered a slight attack.

The young worked heroically in the sacristy in the preparation of funeral ceremonies which were sometimes repeated three times a day and in the care given the dying.

The saint never refused anyone. Should someone inconveniently interrupt her, she immediately rendered service with such grace that it looked as if she owed the person. At times one could be deceived by her obliging nature.

The prioress's feast day drawing near, some of the religious asked Therese to embellish their gifts with her paint brush. Sometimes a sister found her decoration less attractive than another, the artist reaping trouble instead of thanks.

To satisfy an ingrate religious without the least objection, the servant of God painted inartistic subjects because her companion suggested it be done this way.

Accustomed to being served, this same sister never hesitated to ask favors of Therese, even when she was fevered and hemorrhaging.

The angelic nun held that the more repugnant a person, the more one must show kindness toward that person. Celine evidenced this.

"One day," she said, "my sister—in order to encourage me in a similar difficulty—acknowledged to me the violence that she did to herself for a long time, in order to overcome an antipathy.

"This confidence was a revelation to me because she mastered herself to a point where nothing seemed an effort for her; and I was even more dumbfounded when she told me the name of the Sister who was the occasion of her daily struggles.

"In reality, I found the servant of God so amiable and so obliging towards this Sister, that I would have taken her for her best friend."[11]

St. Therese of the Child Jesus even sacrificed her spiritual interests to the service and pleasure of others.

"I have seen her," attested Sr. Genevieve of the Holy Face, "finding a book from which she was deriving much good and passing it on to the Sisters with the result that she never finished reading it in spite of her desire to do so."

During group work, reports her biographer, she took her place near those religious who seemed sad.[12] Not breaking the rule of silence, she at least smiled at them affectionately praying that Jesus would console them.

In the parlor, although the saintly child permitted her older sisters to do the talking, her respected judgment often caused her to be selected as arbitrator in slight disagreements. Because of Therese's compassion, each one confided willingly her domestic troubles.[13]

When failing to restore courage to the afflicted, she recommended their souls to our Lord. Usually her prayers were granted.

The charity of the saint even extended to the workmen who sometimes came to the cloister. Unable to address them directly, she gave them medals which they wore on their clothing.

The charity of Therese influenced all souls—even beyond the monastery—sanctifying them, comforting them, saving them.

Upon being appointed novice mistress, the holy Carmelite became even more charitable to these young souls. She forbade their quibbling and disputing, reminding them of the sentence

in the *Imitation,* "It is better to leave each one to his own thinking than to give way to contentious discourses."[14]

"God will not ask us to give an account of our knowledge, but
of our virtue," she said. "It is then preferable to allow foolish
things to be said or done rather than to fail in charity."

She counseled her novices to make use of recreation, not for
relaxation, but in order to gladden one's neighbor. The apostolate of joy! Sweetly, she practiced it.

"It is not necessary to let your little faults be known in this
manner," she said to a young, crying sister. "Nothing casts so
much gloom over community life. I want you always to have a
calm and peaceful face like a little child who is always happy.

"I am joyful and happy, even when I am suffering. We read in
the lives of certain saints that they were grave and austere, even
at recreation. These attract me less than Theophane Venard
who was always and everywhere happy."[15]

At recreation, she cheered even the most taciturn by her
charm and lively spirit.

"Where, then is Sr. Therese of the Child Jesus?" they would
ask when she was delayed.

If she was tending other duties and could not come, they
would say, "Then, we are not going to laugh today!"[16]

Even her lingering illness did not drown the spontaneous
laughter of her childlike character. In the infirmary one evening
Mother Agnes of Jesus and her other two sisters grew drowsy.
Slyly, the saint watched.

"Peter, James, and John!" she said to them with a piquant
smile as they woke up.

Another time, the infirmary attendant had trapped a mouse.
Behind Therese's bed, she quietly conferred with another sister
on how to dispose of it.

At that moment a novice was crying for the sufferings of St.
Therese of the Child Jesus. Therese, wishing to divert her attention, motioned to the young sister and whispered in her ear, "Do
you hear the fuss about that mouse? Go and find the poor little

beast and put it here beside me; the doctor will be here soon, and I will be examined with a stethoscope and attended to; we'll see which of the two invalids will be cured first."

In another instance, after a serious conversation on holy poverty, she exclaimed, "Holy Poverty! A holy thing that will not get into heaven, isn't it strange."[17]

Spirited laughter followed. Therese, happy at distracting her peers, looked cheerful.

When her sisters expressed sadness at seeing her condition worsen each day, she told them, "In the face of sickness, one must be cheerful; we must not grieve like a person who has no hope . . . you'll end up by making me sorry to be alive."

"Oh!—we'll draw good out of evil!"

Mischievously, Therese said, "Truthfully, though, I only said that to frighten you!"

Her sister, Sr. Marie of the Sacred Heart said to her, "The thought that you are going to die throws me into such a state of grief that if I listened to myself, I would speak to no one."

Therese answered, "That would not be the spirit of the gospel. No matter what the circumstance, we must be all things to all men."

A soul so charitable to the living, must likewise be charitable to the dead. Here she lacked nothing.

The servant of God uttered the heroic act favoring the souls in purgatory. In the hands of the Blessed Virgin, she placed the expiatory and satisfactory part of her daily merits, so they could be applied to them. Many times a week she piously made the way of the Cross for the dead, reciting each day six Our Fathers and Hail Marys.[18]

One day, fever and oppression reducing her to exhaustion, she asked to continue this practice.

On one of her last days, she said to the infirmary attendant, "Give me, I beg of you, a crucifix so that I may kiss it in order to gain a plenary indulgence for the souls in purgatory. I can no longer give them anything else!"

Sr. Marie of the Sacred Heart said to her, "How happy one must be to die after having spent her life in loving!"

With a heavenly expression, the saint answered her, "Yes, but to taste this happiness, one must first have practiced fraternal charity."

Since during her lifetime she had faithfully fulfilled the divine precept, St. Therese of the Child Jesus reaped salutary fruits.

"Oh, Jesus," she wrote, "'charity gladdens my heart.' Since that sweet flame consumes me, I run with delight in the way of Your 'new commandment'; and I wish to keep on running until the blessed day when, uniting myself to the virginal cortege, I will follow You into boundless space, singing Your new canticle, which must be that of love!"

Practical Application

Christ's outline of the last judgment warns us that fraternal charity will be principal.

Let us be careful, then, not to abuse our neighbor for fear of being stranded "on the side of the goats." There we will be eternally deprived of the sight of God and the company of our saint, since without doubt she will be "among the sheep."[19]

We have shown that St. Therese of the Child Jesus had admirable charity. This is most important.

God cannot be pleased with worshippers who tear to pieces the reputation of their neighbor. Are we not commanded, "Go and be reconciled with your brother first and then come back and offer your gift"?[20]

We must form kind thoughts not only to sanctify ourselves but to save ourselves.

Let us avoid faults, let us excuse the weak and culpable, and may our only retaliation against our enemies consist in praying for and serving them. Then we can consider ourselves among the true disciples of little Therese.

"May you be angels of peace and not justices of peace," she recommended to her novices.

Let us imitate the servant of God in her universal charity for the poor, the sick, the afflicted, the agonizing, and the dead. Does not faith teach us that most of these souls remain in the fires of purgatory?

We can easily comfort them through Mass, Communion, way of the Cross, plenary and partial indulgences, and church visits.[21]

Why do we so rarely do it, or not do it at all?

When we are making expiation in that prison of fire, we will be comforted if some charitable person comes to our aid. But should we not fear that God will punish us for our indifference to others?

May this uncertainty make us reflect seriously and make us more charitable in the future.

COLLOQUY: With the holy souls in purgatory. Six Our Fathers and six Hail Marys for their deliverance.

> The principle plenary indulgence which everyone can gain without the ordinary conditions is the indulgence "of charity which covers a multitude of sins."[22]
>
> *St. Therese of the Child Jesus*

Notes

1. Ps. 133:1.
2. *Vie de Sainte Therese de l'Enfant Jesus,* p. 219.
3. *L'Esprit de Ste. Therese de l'Enfant Jesus,* p. 174.
4. *Summarium of 1919,* p. 501.
5. Matt. 25:36.
6. *Summarium of 1919,* p. 559.
7. *Histoire d'une Ame,* Ch. 12, p. 229.

8. Mark 15:29.

9. Crucified Jesus was looked upon with mockery and malice whereas on the part of this visitor there was only a good intention expressed a little foolishly. Therese was too upright not to perceive the difference in making the comparison.

10. Luke 12:37.

11. *Summarium of 1919,* p. 604.

12. *Child Jesus,* Laveille, p. 271.

13. Ibid., p. 284.

14. *Imitation of Christ,* 3, ch. 44, v. 1.

15. *Summarium of 1919,* p. 565.

16. *L'Esprit de Ste. Therese de l'Enfant Jesus,* pp. 210–211.

17. Ibid., p. 211.

18. The following decree concerning plenary indulgences was promulgated by His Holiness Pius IX on April 14, 1856. One can gain a plenary indulgence each time one recites six Our Fathers and Hail Marys for the intentions of the Sovereign Pontiff.

19. Matt. 25:33.

20. Matt. 5:24.

21. The Portiuncula, the feast of Our Lady of the Rosary, of Our Lady of Mt. Carmel—under the usual conditions.

22. Proverbs, 10:12.

Chapter Six
Her Humility

O You, Who by a single work can all the world delight,
Are pleased to hide Your profound wisdom, prudence, might,
  So as to appear ignorant!
  O Lord omnipotent,
    Remember!

St. Therese of the Child Jesus

St. Bernard points out two degrees of humility: to bear affronts patiently and to remain unassuming in prosperity and honors.

Continually exercising, Therese became perfectly humble. Neither the intoxication of praise nor the cooling waters of defeat had the power to upset the serenity of her soul.

Her humility in the midst of contempt

"Humiliation is the only way to sainthood," declared the servant of God.

From adolescence, she dreamed of St. John of the Cross. "Lord, to suffer and to be despised for You!" God saw to it that this was fully realized in her.

The trial of sensitiveness, through which she passed from age four to fourteen, made her powerless, morally inferior. She became permanently humiliated, so passionately was she taken up with this ideal. Her mind seemed blurred by a mist of melancholy.

59

"I heard the intelligence of others being praised frequently," she acknowledged, "but never mine so I concluded I had none.

"I needed this austere formation, more than if I had not been insensible to praise."

When Therese came to Carmel, she found there an impenetrable fortress. Monsignor Delatroette, the rigid superior, refused her admittance on account of her age.

He could not help being vexed when, on the order of Bishop Hugonin, he was constrained to admit her the following year.

"Very well, Reverend Mothers," he said dryly, "You can sing a Te Deum. As delegate of His excellency, the Bishop, I present to you this fifteen-year-old child, whose entrance you have so desired. I hope that she won't disappoint your expectations; but let me remind you that if it turns out otherwise, you alone will be responsible."[1]

The sisters were stunned by this unfounded position. Mother Mary of Gonzaga was impressed by the monseigneur's peevishness and so tested the young aspirant on every occasion.

Meeting Therese who had been pulling up weeds, she said brusquely, "Why, this child does absolutely nothing! . . . what is this that a novice has to be sent for a walk every day?"

Another time, noticing a cobweb, she exclaimed in front of the whole community, "It's easy to see that our cloisters are being swept by a fifteen-year-old child! . . . What a pity! Go quickly to remove that cobweb and learn to be more careful in the future."

"And in everything," said the saint, "that's how she always acted where I was concerned."

Mother Agnes of Jesus, silent and compassionate witness to these injustices, confided later to her little sister, "Oh! how I pitied you at the time!"

Like a valiant soldier who makes light of his wounds and shows his healed scars, Therese answered, "It was not necessary, I assure you, to have pitied me so much. I rose so high above all those things that I was fortified by humiliations; there was no one braver than I in the battle."

So she would not be prey to flattery, she gave the reason for her bravery.

"I was always being told that I had courage; and there is so little truth to it that I told myself: 'why, people must not lie like that!' and I was determined with the help of grace to acquire courage.

"I was like a warrior who, upon being congratulated for his bravery and knowing very well that he is only cowardly, would end up by being embarrassed at the compliments and wishing that he did not merit them."

Despite the humiliations which were her daily bread, the serenity of the novice remained unchanged.

Far from spurning these humiliations, she repeated with the psalmist, "It is good for me, O Lord, that You have humiliated me."[2] But it was not without many valiant struggles that she conquered her pride completely.

Once, one of her companions accusing her of a fault, Therese experienced such a desire to justify herself that she had to flee as a last resort.

When the mistress of novices admonished her for a negligence of which she was not guilty, she kissed the ground and promised to be more careful in the future.

The little saint did not excuse herself because the rule of Carmel forbids it. But early in her religious life, it cost her much. "I had to keep calling to mind that at the last judgment everything would be made known."

Later these desires of justification seemed childish to her.

A young sister once said to her, "When someone reproaches me, I would rather deserve it than be accused unjustly."

"Well, I prefer to be wrongly accused," answered St. Therese of the Child Jesus, "because then I have nothing to reproach myself for and I offer that to the good God with joy; then I humble myself in thinking that I could very well be capable of doing what I was accused of."

Far from fearing contemptuous treatment, she desired it.

"If I had not been allowed to stay in Carmel," she confided, "I would have sought admission into some refuge as a penitent in order to live there unknown and despised."

During her retreat before profession, she gained new humility.

"Contempt had an attraction for me," she wrote Mother Agnes of Jesus, "but at present, I am passionately fond of being forgotten." The predestined one had the opportunity to fully satisfy this attraction, because there were times when she was practically ignored.

She never had a voice at the chapter in her monastery. And although she was certainly mistress of novices, she was never given the title and was considered until the end only the senior in the novitiate. Like St. John of the Cross, of whom many of his contemporaries said "he is a somewhat out of the ordinary religious," Therese was so insignificant in the community that certain sisters, upon seeing her ill, asked what could possibly be written about her in an obituary.[3]

Her illness made her even more of an outcast.

"They have relieved me of every occupation. I thought my death would not cause the least disturbance in the community," she confided.

"Doesn't it bother you to look like a useless member of the community?"

"Oh! no, that's the least of my worries."

This apparent useless member was in reality the treasure of the Lisieux Carmel. But a few resentful religious delighted in slighting her to the end.

One of them, a lay sister in charge of the infirmary one day, offered the saint, then suffering a grave attack, a nourishment which would surely have provoked vomiting. Therese refused it sweetly, pointing out the danger of accident.

The sister made this unkind reflection. "I don't know why they talk so much about Sr. Therese of the Child Jesus; she does nothing remarkable; it cannot even be said that she is exactly a good religious."

After hearing of this, Therese responded with a smile. Later a sister of proven virtue came to see her, and she confided to her the joy of her misjudged soul.

"To hear on my deathbed that I am not even a good religious," she said, "what joy!"[4]

We have admired the humility of Therese when met with contempt. Now let us look at her surrounded with respect.

Certain sisters were so taken up with the merits of Therese that her virtue could not fail to excite these impartial, discerning religious. It was evident that they esteemed her.

A twenty-year-old nun would not have been selected to head the formation of novices if they had not found exceptional aptitudes in her.

"If I was looked upon in the community as an incompetent religious, lacking intelligence and judgment, it would be impossible, Mother, for me to help you," she said to her prioress.

However, the confidence her superiors placed in her did not make her vain, since former rebuffs remained etched in her memory.

"The little flower preserves in her calyx precious drops from the roses of humiliation received in bygone days," she wrote in her poetic language.

This remembrance served her well because, notwithstanding her natural qualities, she was also endowed with good looks which, even in Carmel, attracted too much flattery.

Therese missing recreation one day, the mother prioress and some of the other sisters alluded to her beauty and refinement. When this remark was told Therese, she replied, "Ah! what is that to me? Less than nothing; it's boredom! When one is so near death, she cannot rejoice in such trifles!"

Praise concerning the depth of her spirituality no longer made an impression on her either. One day someone applied to her this saying of St. John of the Cross. "Souls, having arrived at perfect love are able to see their supernatural beauty without any danger to themselves."

She replied, "What beauty? I do not see my beauty at all. I see only the graces I have received from God."

"You are really a saint!" said one novice of her.

"No," she quickly replied, "I have never performed the deeds of the saints. I am only a very little soul whom the good God has laden with graces . . . in heaven you will see that I am telling you the truth."

"We shall find your body incorrupt."

"Oh! no, that would be to depart from my little way of humility."

"They will always find me imperfect; whereas with you, they see only virtue in you!" sighed a young sister.

"Perhaps that is because I have never desired it," answered her angelic mistress. "But you are wrong in fretting because your victory consists precisely in being considered imperfect. The unfavorable opinion of creatures takes nothing from you and it makes you acquire humility."

"You are very privileged," the novices said to her, "in being chosen to point out to souls the way of childhood."

"Why would I want God to be served by me rather than by another?" she asked. "The instrument is of little importance provided His reign is established in souls."

St. Therese had acquired such humility that she attained absolute forgetfulness of self. With simplicity, she repeated with the psalmist, "Lord, my life is as nothing before You."[5]

When Mother Agnes of Jesus told her that, after her death her virtues would be highly valued, the saint immediately channeled all the praise toward the God who had sanctified her.

"It is God alone Who will have to be valued," she said, "because there is nothing valuable in my little nothingness."

Another time when her sister was feeling in low spirits—she

said to Therese, "Alas! I will have nothing to give to God at my death; my hands will be empty and that troubles me very much."

Therese answered. "Well! we're both in the same boat; but you are not like me. Even if I should accomplish all the works of St. Paul, I would still believe that I am 'an unprofitable servant'; I would find myself with empty hands; but that is just the thing which gives me joy because, having nothing, I receive all from God."

She was by no means puffed up from the good work she did with her novices.

"Our Lord has a particular love for you since He confides other souls to you," one of her daughters said to her.

St. Therese answered humbly, "It is not because He wants me to serve you as His interpreter that He loves me more; rather, it is because He makes me your little servant."

The young mistress tired quickly of the praises from her daughters, as from an overly-sweet food. She preferred reproaches symbolized "by a fine little salad well vinegared, well spiced." So God, always wishing to satisfy her, served her a repugnant dressing now and then from some little postulant. Therese was delighted with this.

One of the older sisters served her with her special dish when she said to her ill-humoredly, "Instead of forming novices at your age you are very much in need of being directed yourself."

The saint accepted this humiliation with delight.

"Oh! Sister," she answered, "you are so right; I am more imperfect than you think!"

Once, when a religious confided to St. Therese her fears concerning humility, the saint answered, "I, too, have many weaknesses but I am never surprised at them. I am not always so prompt to rise above earthly trifles as I would like; for example, sometimes I am tempted to be upset over a silly little thing I said or did. Then I'll take hold of myself and say: 'Alas! I am still at the starting point!' But I tell myself this in great peace, without sadness. When we gently accept the humiliation of being imperfect, God's grace immediately comes to our aid."

Such a humble soul could resign herself to writing her autobiography only on the order of her prioress. To a companion who was intent on imitating her, she said, "Be careful about that. As far as I am concerned, I would not want to write anything about my life without a special obedience, and an obedience that I would never seek. It is more humble to write nothing about oneself."[6]

One day, when Mother Agnes of Jesus was talking with her about the manuscript and the public edification that would come of it, she answered, 'Ah! everyone will see that it all comes from God! The fact that I will get glory from it will be a gratuitous gift which will not belong to me; yes, everyone will be convinced of it."

Humility for Therese was a sort of mysterious Samson's hair in which her strength resided. She was convinced that the edifice of her perfection would crash as soon as she began to trust herself.

"If I had voluntarily entertained a proud thought," she said, "for example, something like this: 'I have acquired such and such a virtue; I'm certain of being able to practice it.' Or if I say 'O my God, You know that I love You too much to dwell upon a single thought against faith,' my temptations would become so violent that I would certainly succumb to them. Indeed, in this case, I would be trusting to my own strength; and when that happens we risk falling into the abyss."

Avoiding this moral catastrophe, whose danger is no more unnatural than the fall of the angels from heaven for a single proud thought, the Lord granted his little servant humility to the end of her life.

The blessed sacrament being brought her one morning in the infirmary, the community reciting the confiteor, Therese was seized with a sense of unworthiness.

When she finished her thanksgiving, she said to Mother

Agnes of Jesus, "I saw Our Lord there ready to give Himself to me, and I found that confession so necessary! I felt like the Publican, a great sinner; and I found God so merciful! When I felt the sacred species on my lips, I wept! ... I honestly believe that I have shed tears of perfect contrition." Adding in a moving voice, "It is impossible to say that such sentiments come from oneself; it is the Holy Spirit alone Who can produce them in the soul!"[7]

Admiring the virtues of the dying nun, Mother Agnes of Jesus wanted others outside the monastery to profit by them—even the doctor of the community, Monsieur de Corniere, who attended her. To this end, she urged St. Therese of the Child Jesus to say a few words of edification to him. But Therese resisted this form of spiritual pretension.

"Mother," she said, with the openness of a small child, "that's not my way; let M. de Corniere think what he wants. I love only simplicity, and have a horror of anything to the contrary. I assure you that if I do what you wish, it would be wrong on my part."

But if evangelical simplicity prevented the servant of God from posing as a preacher for the doctor, this same simplicity pointed up her humility and gratitude.

"Mother," she said to Mother Agnes of Jesus, "if you wish, after my death to show my gratitude to Dr. de Corniere who took care of me, you can give him a picture with these words on it: 'What you have done to the least of these my little ones, you have done to Me.'"[8]

How can one describe Therese's repentance when, through inadvertence, she caused someone pain?

"I have seen her," attested Mother Agnes of Jesus, "asking pardon with touching humility of Sisters whom she believed she had offended."

One day when she was extremely weak she became vexed at being misunderstood, immediately calling for the infirmary attendant.

"Oh! I beg you to forgive me!" she said. "Pray for me!" Tears of repentance ran down her pale cheeks.

A few minutes later, she confided to her little mother, "How happy I am to have the feeling of being so imperfect and to need so much the mercy of God at the moment of death. It is so peaceful to feel weak and helpless." With such dispositions, she set sail for eternity.

"I have never desired human glory. The glory of my Jesus is my only ambition; I abandon my glory to Him. And if He seems to forget me—well! He is free, since I no longer belong to myself but to Him."

It is sublime to be exalted by God. The very glory Therese refused is what Jesus poured on his beloved spouse in proclaiming her holy before heaven and earth. Was the little flower elated by this triumph? No.

"All creatures could bow to me, admire me, overwhelm me with their praises; that would not add one shadow of vain satisfaction to the real joy which I experience at seeing myself in the eyes of God a poor little nothing and nothing more!"

In view of the glory bestowed upon her, can we not say that the prophecy of the Magnificant is realized to the letter for this little one."

"He has put down the mighty from their seat, and has exalted the humble."[9]

Practical Application

No practical inference appears more opportune than those furnished by the servant of God in correspondence with her family.

In 1897 she wrote Celine, "Sometimes we are taken by surprise in desiring great things. Then humbly we rank ourselves among the imperfect, esteeming ourselves little souls whom God must sustain at each moment.

"As soon as He sees that we are fully convinced of this, He

holds out His hand to us. But if, under the pretext of zeal, we wish to rise, He leaves us to ourselves. It is enough to humble oneself, to bear our imperfections patiently; that is genuine sanctity as far as we are concerned."

A few lines to her cousin Marie Guerin gives us some insight into the state of a truly humble soul.

"You are deceived, my dear," she wrote, "if you think that Therese walks the path of sacrifice spiritedly: she is weak, very weak; and each day she finds it a new and salutary experience. But Jesus is happy to acquaint her with the science 'of boasting in her weakness.' This is a great grace, and I ask Him to give it to you because in this sentiment is found peace and tranquility of heart. When she sees herself so destitue, she no longer takes much account of herself, but looks only to her well-Beloved."[10]

Let us be attentive and meditate on these two fragments of her letters. Let us put them into practice and we will be surprised at the marvelous progress we will make in virtue, because it is an established fact "that God resists the proud but gives His graces to the humble."[11] May He be praised forever!

COLLOQUY: With Jesus, Meek and Humble of Heart.

> On this strange shore, O Jesus, for me
>   What contempt did You bear anew?
> I wish to humble myself for Thee
> In all things the lowest, the least to be
>   O Jesus, for You.
>
> *St. Therese of the Child Jesus*

Notes

1. Deposition of Mother Agnes of Jesus at the apostolic process, p. 162.
2. Ps. 119:71.

3. *L'Esprit de Sainte Therese de l'Enfant Jesus*, p. 166.
4. *Summarium of 1919*, p. 573.
5. Ps. 39:5.
6. *Summarium of 1919*, p. 724.
7. Ibid., p. 310.
8. Matt. 25:40.
9. Luke 1:52.
10. *Vie Complete de Ste. Therese de l'Enfant Jesus*, letter dated in the year 1894, p. 864.
11. I Peter, 5:5.

Chapter Seven
Her Spirit of Prayer

I can obtain all things when in secrecy
My heart speaks to the Heart of my King
This sweet prayer, in such mystery
Is heaven for me!

St. Therese of the Child Jesus

The spirit of prayer of St. Therese of the Child Jesus is characterized by five distinct features: (a) boldness; (b) simplicity; (c) supernatural eminence; (d) constancy; (e) efficacy.

The boldness of her prayer

Little Therese was only twenty-two months old when Madame Martin announced to her elder daughters, "She prays like a little angel; it is extraordinary!"

When she was five, Therese's soul was already attracted to contemplation. While M. Martin fished silently along the banks of the Toques River, Therese sat by herself.

"Then," she wrote, "my thoughts became very deep and without knowing what it was to meditate, my soul was plunged into real prayer. Earth seemed to me a place of exile and I dreamed of heaven."

"She talks only of God," wrote Madame Martin at this time. "It is amusing to hear her recite this little rhyme: 'Little child with the golden hair,/Where is God? I am asking you./In all the

71

world—He is everywhere/And high above in the heavens blue!'
When she comes to these last words, she turns her face upwards
with an angelic expression; it is so beautiful that we never grow
tired of hearing her recite it."[1]

Some years later, the games Therese played with her little
cousin Marie, the future Sr. Marie of the Eucharist, revealed the
attractions of the future Carmelites. They imagined themselves
two hardworking, poor, penitent anchorites. One prayed, the
other worked. They changed places from time to time with the
understanding of perfect religious.

Walking together, the two hermits said the rosary on their
fingers, hiding their devotion. Nevertheless, many passersby
smiled at their behavior.

Recollecting, they did not even allow themselves to cry out
when tumbling headlong into a basket of wares owned by a
grocer, unappreciative of their untimely intrusion.

The grocer picking up his scattered articles of produce,
screaming offenses, the frightened solitaries took flight, telling
themselves that customs of hermits were not for Lisieux.

Therese was only ten years old when she asked one of her
playmates—the future St. Marie of the Rosary, Benedictine of
Notre Dame du Pré—to explain how to meditate. When Therese
went back home she begged for godmother to allow her to pray
half an hour each day.

Marie did not feel obligated to satisfy Therese's desire, so the
little girl made up for it on holidays by sitting in a corner of her
room behind the bed curtains. There "she thought of God, of
the shortness of life, and of eternity."

Were these not edifying and bold actions for a child her age?

The simplicity of her prayer

In order to talk with God, Therese, even as an adolescent, did
not resort to books of piety with ready-made formulas. Her mistresses noticed that she rarely followed her prayer book for Holy
Mass.[2] Now and then, by a word or a glance, she was brought back

to order. She returned thanks with a smile. But it was apparent that she was held by some heavenly reality. She prayed without "noise of words."[3]

In Carmel, the servant of God fell on the simplest books. *The Imitation of Christ* and *The Foundations of the Spiritual Life*, with their commentaries, were her delight.

The treatise of Monsignor de Segur, *Piety and the Interior Life*, charmed her with its simplicity. The holy prelate recommended constant meditation on the Gospels as the surest way to unite with Jesus Christ.

Therese concentrated all her reading on this divine book so that at the end of her life she could say, "I no longer find anything in books; the Gospel is enough for me."

According to Sr. Genevieve of the Holy Face, St. Therese scrutinized the Scriptures like a lover to discover "the character of God."[4]

"She interpreted Holy Scripture with an unheard-of facility," attested one of her novices, Sr. Marie of the Trinity. "These divine books held no secrets from her for she knew how to appreciate the beauty of them thoroughly."[5]

Love for liturgical prayer was instilled in Therese's soul from the day she entered Carmel. She chanted the divine office in choir with incomparable fervor.

When she was eighteen, she had an appreciation for the mystical works of St. Teresa and St. John of the Cross. But later on, spiritual writers left her dry.

"Those scholarly books puzzle my brains," she said frankly, "and if there were no other way of getting to heaven than by reading things I don't understand, I don't think I'd ever get there."

Happily, paradise is "made for children and for those who resemble them."[6] For these young friends of Jesus there are short pathways which meet, as surely as do the steep mountain passes, at the divine crossroad where God waits.

The saint's prayer went in this direction. Without losing herself in random speculation, she prattled with the Most High like a child with its father.

"I act like a little child who does not know how to read," she explained artlessly. "I can tell Him very simply what comes to my mind, and I am sure He understands."

At times she was troubled like all little children, her imagination wandering. People benefited from it, because she immediately prayed for them.

"For the love of God," she avowed, "I accept the wildest thoughts which come to my mind."

At other times the young Carmelite, up at five o'clock every morning, became drowsy. Then she would fall asleep like a child in its father's arms.

"I ought to be grieved at falling asleep so often during my prayers and thanksgivings," she said, "but I am not troubled about it.

"I feel that little children are just as pleasing to their parents when they are asleep as when they are awake; and that doctors must put their patients to sleep in order to operate on them; just so: 'the Lord knows what we are made of, He remembers that we are dust.'"[7]

When Therese prayed, she did not become entangled in enumeration.

"If I outlined in detail to God all the needs which souls have entrusted to me," she wrote, "the days would not be long enough. So one morning after communion our Lord gave me an inspiration, and showed me a very simple way of meeting my obligations."

After that, It was sufficient for her to repeat the words, "Draw me and we shall run in your footsteps."[8]

"A soul drawn knows only how to run," she maintained. "All the souls which she loves are drawn after her. It is a natural result of her attraction towards God."

When someone asked her in her last illness, "How is your spiritual life coming along?" the servant of God answered, "My spiritual life at this moment? Why, it is very simple to suffer, and that is all. I do not make any special intention since I have given all my sufferings to God to do with them as it pleases Him."

"But what do you do when someone insists that you pray for such and such a person?"

"I say very simply to God: 'My God, give that soul all that I desire for it.'"

Such was the exquisite simplicity Therese had with the Most High.

The supernatural eminence of her prayer

Spiritual writers agree that mystical states are characterized by three stages: the purgative, the illuminative, and the unitive.

Did St. Therese of the Child Jesus follow this classic course? It seems she did.

In *Les Ascensions de l'ame dans la Bienheureuse Therese de l'Enfant Jesus*, the Reverend Theodore of St. Joseph proved that the holy nun—after mounting the steps leading to acquired and infused prayer and submitting to the purifications of sense and spirit—arrived at transforming union, the summit of mystical prayer.

Three instances verify this.

(a) In her autobiography the saint confided, "Even if I open the most beautiful and touching book, my heart is soon dried up and I read without being able to understand; or if I do understand, my mind is blocked and I cannot meditate."

Isn't that the impotence, manifested in the understanding of the mystics, which is a sure sign of their being called to passive prayer?

(b) Contrary to human action, it is a fact that the graces of which God is the author ordinarily envelop the soul unawares even outside the exercises of piety.

The same went for Therese.

"Divine lights did not often break in upon me during the hours of prayer," she wrote, "but in the middle of my daily occupations."

This passage, observes the Bishop of Bayeux, shows how Therese had acquired the habit of passive contemplation in which God, independent of the soul's effort, transforms it, makes himself its master, and reveals to it truths which she called "lights."

(c) Two years before Therese's death, it seems that the grace of union had been almost permanently granted her.

"She was so united to God that it is said she saw God constantly," Mother Agnes of Jesus testified.

Therese herself revealed, "I do not know what more I will have in heaven than I have now; I shall see God, that is true; but as for being with Him, I am already entirely with Him here on earth."

Someone could object by saying that her faith was obscured the last eighteen months of her life. But those to whom Therese confided believed that these shadows, while purifying her, brought her to the habitual thought of God.

Her helplessness ruffled only the surface. In the depths of her soul, she experienced divine contact with her beloved. It was a heart to heart contact in the night, face to face in the darkness.

One day, alluding to this duality of delight and torment, she said, "I have just read a beautiful passage from *The Imitation*: 'Our Lord, in the garden of Olives, was in possession of all the delights of the Trinity while at the same time suffering the most cruel agony.' It is a mystery, but I assure you that I understand something of it because I am going through it myself."

Another time, as she spoke on the subject of a soul consumed with divine charity, someone quoted to her, "They who surrender themselves to love die in wonderful joy and delightful ecstasy."

She sighed and said, "One must be careful to note that joy and transports of love are found in the depths of the soul only; as for the rest, it still does not prevent me from suffering."

Mystical states are distinguished by extraordinary grace and charisma.

In the life of St. Therese of the Child Jesus miraculous events are rare because, in principle, the way of childhood excludes such phenomena. Enough exist, though, to clearly indicate the mark of the supernatural on this privileged soul.

In the first place, recall the apparition of the Holy Virgin who came to cure a ten-year-old Therese of an illness which the doctors judged incurable.[9]

The servant of God tells us in her autobiography about three mysterious dreams she had.

Again, without attaching extraordinary importance to it. Let us consider the symbolic dreams of many holy persons mentioned in Scripture—such as the dreams of St. Joseph and those of his namesake Joseph, the minister of Pharoah—and not disregard the dreams which the saint shared with us.

The first was a childhood dream in which the sight of cowardly imps made Therese understand the powerlessness of the demons, incapable of sustaining the glance of a soul in the state of grace.

The second concerns the venerable foundress of the Carmel of Lisieux, Mother Genevieve of St. Teresa, who, a few days after her death, appeared in a dream to Therese. She looked upon Therese with tenderness and said to her three times, "To you I bequeath my heart."

Therese tells us about the last dream, the most remarkable of the three.

"On May 10th., at the first glimmer of dawn, while I was asleep it seemed to me that I was walking along a corridor alone with our Mother. All of a sudden and without knowing how I entered, I noticed three Carmelites clothed in their mantles and long veils and I understood that they came from heaven. 'Ah! how happy I would be,' I thought, 'to see the face of one of them!'

"As if my prayer was heard, the tallest of the Saints came towards me and I fell on my knees. O what happiness! She raised her veil—or rather lifted it—and covered me with it. Without any hesitation I recognized the Venerable Mother Anne of Jesus, Foundress of Carmel in France. Her face was beautiful with an immaterial beauty; no light shone upon it and yet, in spite of the thick veil which enveloped both of us, I saw this heavenly countenance illuminated with an ineffably sweet light which seemed to come from itself. The saint covered me with caresses and, seeing how tenderly I was loved, I dared to utter these words: 'O Mother, I beg of you to tell me if God will leave me long on earth? Will He not come to take me soon?'

"She smiled tenderly: 'Yes, soon, very soon . . . I promise you.'

"'Mother,' I added, 'tell me further if God does not want something other than my poor actions and my desires; is He pleased with me?'

"At that moment, the face of the Venerable Mother shone with a new brightness and her expression seemed unbelievably tender:

"'God asks nothing else of you,' she said to me. 'He is pleased, very pleased! . . .'

"And taking my head in her hands, she lavished upon me such caresses that it would be impossible for me to convey the sweetness of it."

Although few in number, these prophetic lights with which St. Therese of the Child Jesus was favored are clearly defined.

At about six years old, she had a vision which gave her food for thought.

"Papa was on a trip and not expected back soon," she wrote. "It was about two or three o'clock in the afternoon. I was alone by a window overlooking the big garden when I saw in front of the laundry a man dressed exactly like papa, but very stooped and old . . . I say old in order to describe the general make-up of his appearance because I could not see his face; his head was covered with a heavy veil.

"He came slowly towards me, with a measured step, skirting my little garden. Almost at once, a feeling of terror seized me and I cried out loudly with trembling voice: 'Papa! Papa!'

"But the mysterious person did not seem to hear me; he continued walking without even turning his head and kept on going towards a clump of spruces which divided the main entrance to the garden. I expected to see him reappear on the other side of the big trees; but the prophetic vision had vanished."

Ten years later, when the cerebral disorder of M. Martin became evident, Therese understood this disquieting enigma.

"Ah! I know now," she cried, "it was truly our father whom God had me see, bent with age and wearing on his venerable face and graying head, the sign of his great trial!"

At times the dead seemed to be in touch with the servant of God. After the death of Monsieur Martin, she confided to Celine, "Our dear father makes us feel his presence in a manner which touches me deeply. After a living death of five long years, what joy to find him again as he used to be; and yet, more fatherly!"

St. Therese of the Child Jesus asked and obtained a tangible sign of the immediate entrance of her father into heaven.[10]

In different circumstances, our Lord communicated to the young saint presentiments which fully justified the reality.

One morning during the influenza epidemic, at the signal for rising she had a feeling that something was the matter with her companion Sr. Magdalen. Going to her, she found her dead on her straw mattress.

Concerning her own brief destiny, the angelic nun seemed to have had definite prophetic insights.

On August 19, 1894, the day before Celine joined her in Carmel, she wrote her, "God has granted my dearest wish! Come, let us suffer together. And then Jesus will take one of us and the others will remain for a short time in exile."

God willed that this short time be prolonged, since all of Therese's sisters lived to considerable age.

In April 1895, still in good health, the holy Carmelite made this new disclosure, "I am going to die soon; this will not be for some months yet, but in two or three years at most; I feel it because of what is passing in my soul."

She also foresaw her providential mission.

"Gather these petals carefully," she said one day, "they will give you pleasure later on." They served not only to give pleasure, but to work miracles.

"After my death, the letter box at Carmel will often bring you news of me," she announced to Mother Agnes of Jesus.

Indeed, a daily influx of letters—three postmen were not enough—was received by the mother prioress telling of the miraculous wonders of her dear little queen.

On her deathbed Therese sent an old mother, whom she loved tenderly, this message, "Tell Mother Herman of the Heart of Jesus that during Mass I saw the grave of little Louis very close to that of old P. Corbinelli."

This alluded to the pseudonyms which the good Mother, impressed by reading the biography of St. Louis of Gonzaga, had amiably bestowed upon Therese and herself.

"That's good," answered Mother Herman, very much moved. "Tell Sr. Therese of the Child Jesus that I understand."

This prophecy was actually realized. Mother Herman died within the year, and up until the translation of the remains of Therese, the two graves lay side by side.

Therese had a presentiment that her memoir would be the object of an overall and posthumous tenderness.

"Ah! I know very well," she said with a radiant smile, "the whole world is going to love me!"

She predicted still more—among them, certain details concerning the editing of her autobiography and the name of the chaplain who would succeed the Abbe Youf.[11] These, contrary to public belief, were realized after her death.

We mention again the mystical grace of the fiery dart which was a divine intervention and an ectasy.[12]

Therese, after rendering an account of this favor, added, "I understand now what the saints say about those states which they have so often experienced."

During a confidential interview one day Therese forgot her humility.

She described some of her prayers in past summer evenings during the great silence,[13] saying she understood what "flight of the spirit" meant.[14] She spoke of another grace—a grace followed by many days of "quietude"—received in the grotto of St. Magdalen in the monastery garden in July 1889.[15]

"It was like a veil thrown over everything on earth for me," she explained. "I felt entirely hidden under the veil of the Blessed Virgin. At that time, I had charge of the refectory and I remember doing things as if I did not do them; it was as if I was acting with a body not my own. I remained in that state for a whole week.

"It is a supernatural state very difficult to explain. God alone can place us in it and sometimes it is enough to detach a soul from this earth forever."

At her death, the servant of God had a vision. Let us take no notice of that, however, because if her angelic smile had allowed anyone to guess it, her sealed lips took the secret with her to the grave.

Finally, if it is true that Therese did not accomplish great things during her lifetime, she so made up for this after her death that she has been called "the greatest miracle worker of modern times."

The constancy of her prayer

St. Therese of the Child Jesus was not content to dedicate the six or seven hours prescribed by the rule of Carmel to daily prayer. She strove to think uninterruptedly of God.

One day a companion surprised her in her cell while sewing, Therese's face resplendent.

"What are you thinking about?" her visitor asked.

"I am meditating on the 'Pater Noster'," answered the saint, raising her beautiful tear-filled eyes heavenward. "It is so sweet to call God our Father."

She reproved novices who lacked recollection.

"You are too full of distractions. Do you worry about what

goes on in other Carmels? Do their troubles prevent you from praying, from saying prayers?

"Well, then, withdraw yourself even from your personal work. Use the time conscientiously which is prescribed for it, but keep your heart detached."

Efficacy of her prayer

The valiant saint did not confine her prayer life to a self-centered circle. She perceived height and depth.

She began by making an agreement with the church triumphant so not to be reproached for foolishness.

"Adopt me as your child," she said to the inhabitants of the heavenly Jerusalem. "The glory that you will make me acquire will redound to you alone; deign to grant my prayer; obtain for me, I beg of you, your double spirit."[16]

Her prayer rising like incense toward the church triumphant, she spread herself over the church militant; then she descended, refreshing as a rose, on the church suffering.

Using this threefold prayer, she kept in contact with the children of God. The very dogma of the Communion of Saints delighted her.

"It is the will of God," she said, "that in this world souls communicate heavenly gifts to one another through prayer so that when they arrive in the Fatherland, they may be able to recognize each other by love with an even greater affection than that of the most ideal family on earth." Adding, "Oh! that we may understand something of these mysteries later on! How many times have I thought that perhaps I owe all the graces which have been heaped upon me to the entreaties of some little soul whom I will know only in heaven!"

If Therese thought she received much more than others, she gave still more. Her trust in the service of God clearly manifested itself.

A single prayer on her part was for many souls the starting point of a tremendous change.

One novice desired that her worldly sister join her in Carmel. Seeing her desire materialize in a dream, the young sister confided it to her holy mistress who told her, "We must get to work, and pray very hard; what a joy it will be if, at the end of Lent, we are heard."

The Lord did not resist the prayers of the two nuns. At the end of Lent the little vocation dream came true.

Spurred on by this sweet experience, the servant of God cried out enthusiastically, "How great is the power of prayer! It is said that a queen always has free access to the king and that she obtains all that she asks."

So God would not resist her prayer, she united it to Jesus Christ. She sang.

> Remember how often the hills You climbed
>   At approach of the setting sun;
> Remember Your prayers so very divine
>   Your songs of love when day was done!
> I offer myself, O my God, with delight
> At prayer—in the Office, morning, noon and night.
>   There so near to Your heart
>   Songs of joy I impart
>   Remember!

This worthy daughter of the illustrious reformer of Carmel disclosed her esteem for the efficacy of prayer.

"A scholar once said: 'Give me a prop, and I will lift the world!' That which Archimedes was not able to obtain, the saints fully achieved. The all-Powerful has given them a prop: He Himself, He alone. For a lever, they possess prayer which flares up into a fire of love. It is thus that 'they have lifted the world'; and the saints still on earth lift it and will continue to lift it until the end of time."

Practical Application

Let us learn from the examples of our heavenly patroness a triple lesson.

The first, when we pray simplicity is in order.

The candor of little children and the humility of the publican pleases God. The prayers and snobbish manners of the pharisees seem pretentious and ridiculous to Him. Christ warned us about it. Let us guard ourselves against this.

Under pretext of simplicity, let us not imagine that it is wrong to use a book while meditating, but pattern our readings after Therese's.

Imitation is not synonymous with mimicking. All is based in principle on the spirit of the amiable saint—the living incarnation of our ideal. We can, we must, safeguard our originality and follow the special way which the Holy Spirit points out to us.

Concerning the most beneficial manner of meditating, we are at times more impressed with the words of spiritual authors than we are with our own often mediocre thoughts. Better to meditatively read than not to meditate at all, dreaming the time idly away.

But if God takes the trouble to instruct us himself, let us close the book. It is fitting that lesser masters hold their peace when the great Teacher speaks.

The second lesson the saint gives us is not to desire extraordinary graces. But if God bestows them on us, receive them with humility.

May we be persuaded that the best meditation is not always that which consoles us most. But certainly that which makes us more watchful, more generous, more humble, more submissive, this is divine.

Third, we must learn to value the spiritual riches of the Communion of Saints.

The learned Tauler made a comment on this subject which St. Therese of the Child Jesus appreciated.

"If I love the good that is in my neighbor more than he loves it himself," he said, "this good is more mine than his. If I love in St. Paul all the favors which God has granted him, they all belong to me by the same right. Through the Communion of Saints I can be rich by all the good that is in heaven, in the angels and in the saints, and in all those who love God."[17]

Like Therese, let us be prudent enough to make friends in high places, so when we die they will receive us into eternity.

Let us unite in a special way with the little queen. She is a member of royalty, and her closeness to us will be sweet and profitable.

Millions of souls experience it daily, among them the Holy Pontiffs themselves.

Vatican delegate to the Lisieux Carmel, The Reverend d'Herbigny, S.J., once said of Pius XI, "He lived in familiar contact with little Therese who obtained many favors for him. He understood so well the method of perfection of the young saint that he held her up as a model for all Christians; and his own personal life mirrored in a delightfully touching manner the same virtues."

May God give us the grace to imitate our holy little friend on earth, so we may have the happiness of resembling her in heaven!

COLLOQUY: With the Holy Spirit

> Sometimes when my soul is so dry that I cannot draw up a single good thought from it, I recite slowly an Our Father and a Hail Mary. These prayers give divine nourishment to my soul and satisfy it.
>
> *St. Therese of the Child Jesus*

Notes

1. Letter to Pauline, March 4, 1877.
2. No one knows why Therese acted in this manner, since in general great profit can be derived in following attentively the liturgical prayers which are the living expression of the Church's thought.
3. *Biography of the Saint,* Monsignor Laveille, p. 107.
4. Deposition at the apostolic process, p. 390.
5. Ibid., p. 702.
6. Matt. 18:3-4.
7. Ps. 103:14.
8. Cant. 1:4.
9. For more details, see Chapter 9, p. 109.
10. A sudden change of heart in a religious very much opposed to the entrance of Celine into the Lisieux Carmel.
11. See Chapter 8, p. 103.
12. See Chapter 4, p. 41.
13. The period of free time and the silence which precedes the recitation of matins.
14. St. Therese, *Chateau de l'Ame, Sixieme Demeure,* Ch. 5.
15. Ibid., *Chemin de la Perfection,* Ch. 33.
16. Allusion to the prayer of the Church asking of Elias "his double spirit."
17. Tauler—Sermon for the 5th Sunday after Pentecost.

Chapter Eight
Her Devotion to Our Lord Jesus Christ

Christ is my love, He is my whole life
He is the Bridegroom Who alone delights me.
St. Therese of the Child Jesus

Therese loved our Lord under every form which his sacred humanity assumed, the little child at Bethlehem and at Nazareth, the man of sorrows in his passion, a heart burning with eternal love. She venerated Him above all in the Holy Eucharist where he perpetuates and culminates his mysteries.

Her devotion to the Infant Jesus

"Oh!" Therese naively told herself, "how happy I would be to bear the name of the Child Jesus in Carmel!"

At nine, Mother Mary of Gonzaga told her, "My dear little one, when you come to us, you will be called Sr. Therese of the Child Jesus."

"In fact, this name suited her so well," observed His Holiness Benedict XV, "that if it had not been given to her providentially her Sisters in religion would have had to bestow it upon her."[1]

From the time of entering the monastery, Therese was given the charge of decorating the statue of the Infant Jesus standing in the cloister. Skillfully arranging flowers and candles, she vividly recalled her Christmas grace of 1886, the two pilgrimages to Loretto, and so many other events dear to her in which the Divine Little King played such an important part.

Had she not been, was she not still, "His little ball," with which he could amuse himself as he pleased—pierce it to see what was inside, throw it into a corner, press it tenderly to his heart?

Her interior life centered around Nazareth, the blessed place where part of the Savior's childhood took place. The mystery of littleness guided her into the assiduous practice of spiritual childhood.

A painting by Celine pictures her on her knees in front of the holy family, assisting the first steps of the little Jesus. Honoring them, Therese scatters roses before them, for which she was always so well known. Then, taking her musical instrument in hand, she sang.

> Jesus, when I see You leave the fond embrace
> Of Your Mother's arms
> To try to walk this earth at trembling pace,
> Your first steps in alarm,
> I'd strew Your path with petals fresh and fair
> Of roses newly clipped
> So that Your tiny feet so tender and so bare
> Would fall on soft and easy step.

Each Christmas her soul overflowed in delightful verse, bits of which her sisters chose at random. The last one which fell to her lot before her sickness went this way:

> I'd like a fruit that is savory,
> A cluster of golden grapes,
> In order to refresh the heavenly King
> And serve His regal taste.
> My Sister, you are the tasty brand;
> You are the grape of His choice.
> Jesus will hold you in His hand
> And delicately press you close.

Was this not the "Veni, Sponsa Christi"[2] of the little Jesus?

Her devotion to the Holy Face

"It was my little Mother," wrote Therese, "who taught me to find the treasures hidden in the Holy Face."

During her retreat before profession, the young Carmelite felt the effects of this discovery.

It was as if Christ took her hand and led her into a sheltered, somewhat darkened passageway, where she soon discerned a veiled brightness which shone about them from the lowered eyes of the face of Jesus.

"What a shame that His eyelids must be lowered," Mother Agnes of Jesus said to her, while they looked upon the traditional visage venerated at tours.

"Oh! no," answered Therese, "it is better this way because since the eyes are the mirror of the soul we would die of joy if we had insight into His Soul. . . .

"Oh! this Holy Face has meant so much in my life! It helped me to compose with ease my Canticle 'To live of love.' In the evening silence, I wrote from memory for three-quarters of an hour the fifteen verses I had composed during the day. That day, on going to the refectory after the examen, I had just composed the stanza: 'To live of love, is to wipe Your Face,/It is to beg pardon for sinners. . . .' I repeated it on passing in front of the picture of the Holy Face which hangs in the gallery. Looking upon it, I shed tears of love."

Not content with lovingly contemplating "this image more beautiful than the lilies and roses of springtime," Therese gathered up the tears like precious pearls which streaked it, so they could be ransomed for souls.

Imitating St. Veronica, she wiped the sweat, dust, spittle, blood, disfiguring that swollen face, so she could hear the prophetic words of Isaias.

"His Face was hidden, He was considered as a man struck by God and brought low."[3]

From that moment, Therese of the Holy Face reflected more on the suffering of her divine spouse than on herself.

"Ah! I would like my face to be hidden like His," she exclaimed, "so that no one would recognize me on earth. I thirst for suffering and to be forgotten."

In dealing with her novices, Therese became the apostle of the holy face—particularly regarding Sr. Genevieve of the Holy Face (Celine, who later reproduced the portrait of our Lord after the manner of the Holy Shroud of Turin, which in 1898 had come to be considered a positive impression.[4]

Chanting the psalms of the office, the servant of God kept an image of the holy face as a bookmark in her breviary. During prayer, she placed it well in view.

On her death bed she pinned it to the curtains. In her agony she often turned the adorable face of the one who had suffered for her.

Her devotion to the sacred heart

The veneration of Therese for the sacred heart of Jesus was more private than that practiced today.

"You know, for my part, I do not see the Sacred Heart like others see it," she wrote Celine, then on pilgrimage to Paray-le-Monial.

"I think quite simply that the Heart of my Spouse is mine alone as mine is His alone, and I speak to Him then in the solitude of this delightful heart-to-heart conversation while waiting to contemplate Him one day without the veil of faith."

She considered devotion to the sacred heart a positive pledge of salvation. "I assure you that God will have pity on her because of her devotion to the Sacred Heart," she said of someone with disconcerting faults.

Speaking of another whose salvation seemed in danger, she said, "Because of her devotion to the Sacred Heart she will be saved though it will be like running through fire."

Her love for the blessed sacrament

At the age of three, the precocious little Therese was already giving her first lesson on eucharistic theology.

"How is it that God can live in such a small host?" asked Celine, then seven years of age.

"That's not surprising," replied Therese, "since God is all-powerful."

"What do you mean by saying He is all-powerful?"

The little Benjamin replied, "I mean that He can do everything He wants to do."

Processions for the Feast of Corpus Christi expanded the heart of this child with untold joy.

"What happiness to scatter flowers along the path of God!" she cried.

Before letting the petals fall, she flung them high. Her happiness could not be expressed when she saw one of the rose petals touch the monstrance.

Young, Therese heard the tender invitation of her divine master. "Let the little children come to me!"[5]

At that time, alas! little children were forbidden to respond to the invitation, because the liberal decree of Pius X had not yet come out.[6]

One Christmas eve, no longer able to restrain herself, she whispered to her godmother, "Oh! please let me go and steal the little Jesus . . . I am so little and there are so many people that nobody will notice me receiving communion."

But Marie objected. Big tears rolled down the child's cheeks when she saw her sisters approach the communion rail.

The little lover of the Eucharist had not yet understood these prophetic words from centuries before. "The days will come when I will send hunger to the earth; not the hunger for bread nor the thirst for water, but hunger for the Word of God."[7]

One day Therese spied Bishop Hugonin escorted by two

vicars general. She started to ask him to advance the date of her first Holy Communion. Again the prudent Marie restrained her.

Three months before the great day, Sr. Agnes of Jesus sent to her Benjamin a manuscript which, under a flowery symbol, hid a serious work.

Therese executed this pious program with so much fervor that at the end of three months "the precious little book of Carmel" showed a splendid record of 815 sacrifices and 2,773 acts of love.

At last, the grandest day of her life came.

"What inexpressible memories linger in my soul of the least details of those heavenly hours," she wrote later. "The joyous awakening in the morning, the reverential and tender affection of the mistresses, the dressing room filled with snow-white outfits in which each child in turn was dressed; above all, the entrance into the chapel and the singing of the morning canticle: 'O Holy Altar, the Angels Surrounding!'"

But this ceremony, already consoling, only preluded another intimate feast.

"Ah! how sweet was the first kiss of Jesus to my soul!" confided the saint. "Yes, it was a kiss of love! I felt myself loved and I said to Him, too: 'I love You, and I give myself to You forever!'

"Jesus asked nothing of me. For a long time, now, He and little Therese looked upon and understood each other... on that day, our meeting could no longer be called a simple glance, but a fusion.[8]

"We were no longer two: Therese had disappeared like a drop of water which is lost in the ocean; Jesus alone remained: He was the Master, the King!"

Her happiness over her first Communion was so profound that she wept. As her companions showed astonishment, she said, "Nobody understands that one cannot bear all the joy of heaven coming into an exiled, weak and mortal heart without bursting into tears."

On the evening of the great day, after visiting Carmel where she caught a glimpse of Sr. Agnes of Jesus, Therese wrote these three resolutions. "1) I will never be discouraged; 2) Everyday I will say a Memorare; 3) I will humble my pride."[9]

Constrained, despite herself, to conform to the somewhat Jansenistic custom of the time, Therese eventually received Communion on the great feasts of the year which, unfortunately, were only too few.

Her confessor, amazed by the purity and fervor of this soul, little by little allowed her to increase her Communions until she was receiving weekly. The young girl carefully prepared herself for them from the evening before, aided by her sister Marie.

One evening Marie spoke to Therese on redemption and suffering, the saint recalling this conversation after Communion the next day. Soon, her heart enflamed with an ardent desire of the cross, she understood that her prayer would be heard.

"Then," she declared, "my soul was filled with consolations such as I have never experienced before in my life."

St. Bonaventure referred to this subject, not regarding the Eucharistic Sacrament itself which always remains the same, rather regarding the manner in which it adapts itself to souls who receive it.

"For the weak," he said, "the Eucharist is a milk which nourishes; for the strong, it is a wine which quickens."

The bread of angels was for Therese a source of delight. Doubtless, divine wisdom applied these condescending words of the Song of Songs to her. "Our sister is still very little."[10] Consequently, they overwhelmed her with spiritual milk.

But in Carmel, Christ considered her strong enough to intoxicate her with the astringent delights of his blood. "The blood of Christ inebriates me."[11] Her aridity in receiving Communion became for her a chalice of sacrifice, sparkling wine quickening the strong.

"What can I say of my thanksgivings here and now?" she said to her prioress. "There is no moment when I am less consoled.

"Distractions and sleep often trouble me, but it is not unusual for me to make the resolution to continue my thanksgiving throughout the entire day since I have made it so badly in choir."

She was not distressed by this troublesome state of soul.

"It is only natural for me to be in aridity," she observed, "since I do not desire the Lord to visit me for my own satisfaction, but solely for His."

St. Therese of the Child Jesus suffered from dryness, but she would not allow it to be said that its cause was a lack of fervor.

Flavoring the monotony of her thanksgivings, she had recourse to delightful ingenuities. For example, she improvised serenades, the saints pious and invisible artists.

The Blessed Virgin was invited to become mistress of the house, making this domicile of fortune resplendent by the charm of her smile, the glitter of her clothing and her jewels.

Therese stayed modestly in the background watching with tenderness the face of Jesus in order to share his joy.

Other times, she pictured her soul "in the disguise of a tiny child three or fours years of age who got her hair and clothing in disarray while playing. But soon the Blessed Virgin came to my rescue," she explained, "and quickly made me take off my dirty apron, rearranged my hair, and adorned it with a pretty ribbon or simply a flower... and that was enough to make me gracious and to admit me without blushing to the Feast of the Angels."

Her thanksgivings were undoubtedly fervent, but the preparation yielded her nothing. During her many sleepless nights, Therese collected her thoughts more carefully, multiplying spiritual communions and sacrifices.

One day at recreation she said to Mother Agnes of Jesus, "Mother, please read to me the letter you have for me. I abstained from asking you for it this afternoon in order to prepare myself for communion tomorrow."

Her fidelity never degenerated into a Jansenistic anxiety which moves away from Jesus on the pretext of incompleteness and unworthiness.

On the contrary, Therese put souls who confided in her on

their guard against scruples, often ill-founded, by which the devil tries to keep them away from Holy Communion.

As early as 1888, she wrote her cousin Marie Guerin, "When the devil has succeeded in keeping a soul away from Holy Communion, he has gained his ends and Jesus weeps. O my little Marie, think that this good Master is there in the tabernacle expressly for you and you alone, that He burns with a desire to come into your heart. No, it is not possible that a heart whose only repose is to contemplate the tabernacle—and it is yours you tell me—offends our Lord to the point of not being able to receive Him. That which offends Jesus, what wounds Him to the heart, is lack of confidence."[12]

Therese wrote to a young sister, who, after committing a fault, wanted to deprive herself of Holy Communion. "Dear little flower of Jesus, it is well enough that, by humiliation, you strike roots in the ground. You must open your corolla a little and raise it very high so that the Bread of Angels may come like a divine dew to strengthen you and to give you everything you lack."

As sacristan, Therese rejoiced at touching the sacred vessels and preparing the linens for the holy sacrifice.

After Mass one day, she noticed a particle of the Host on the paten. Quickly she called some of her companions. In their company she adored the blessed sacrament, then placed the precious fragment at the disposition of the chaplain.

Reverend Father Youf, filling this function and knowing of Therese's attraction for frequent Communion, was sorry that he could not allow her to receive every day. Mother Mary of Gonzaga, standing firm on the rights which monastic traditions in France conferred on superiors at the time, remained inflexible. However, in 1892, when influenza broke out in the community, the confessor comforted Therese each morning with the Holy Eucharist. This privilege lasted several months, even after the epidemic ceased.

"How sweet it was," cried Therese, "I never asked for this

exception but I was very happy to be united each day with my Beloved."

She had an intuition that our Lord desires, even more than we ourselves, to be united to us daily.

"It is not to remain in the golden ciborium that Jesus comes down from heaven each day," she said, "but to find another heaven, the heaven of our soul where He takes His delight."[13]

Despite the brief of Leo XIII which transferred to the confessor the right to regulate the number of Communions, the servant of God never consistently obtained daily Communion. But she obtained it for her community after her death, foretelling of this to Sr. Marie of the Sacred Heart.

"There will come a time when our chaplain will be Father Hodierne," she told her, "and he himself will give us Holy Communion every day."

At that time neither the death nor the replacement of Father Youf was foreseen. Nor was there any known circumstance to account for the nomination of the priest designated by the young wonder-worker.

Nevertheless, a few days after Therese's death, her prediction was realized. On October 15, 1897 the new chaplain of Carmel chose as the text for his first sermon these words, "Come and eat My Bread."[14] It was an invitation to daily Communion that he extended to the religious.[15]

During her last illness, the heroic little saint dragged herself to Holy Communion when it was offered, greatly fatiguing herself, bringing tears to the eyes of those who knew her state.

"Therese never believed anything was too great a price to pay for the happiness of being united to her God," attested one of her sisters.

Once bedridden, the sacred species, small as it was, was too big for her to swallow easily. Mother Agnes urging that it be made smaller, the servant of God said to her, "Thank you for having asked that I be given only a small particle of the sacred species. I still had great difficulty in swallowing it, but how happy I was to have God in my heart! I cried with joy as I did on the day of my First Communion."

Was it not martyrdom when the spitting of blood and persistent suffocation deprived her of the bread of angels the last five weeks of her life?

Famished for the Eucharist, she repeated, "I cannot live without You, Jesus, nor can I do without the sweetness of Your visits."[16]

Nevertheless, she humbly accepted this painful privation.

"I cannot receive Holy Communion as often as I want to, but Lord, are You not All-Powerful? Remain in me as in a tabernacle; never withdraw Yourself from Your little victim!"

During the tedious waiting preceding the Communion of the divine priest, Therese, his little victim, rested peacefully on the paten.

At last the divine high priest took her, bending down, absorbing her, transforming her into one of praise for eternity.

Practical Application

The liturgical cycle leads us through Christmas in December, through Easter in the spring, to the Sacred Heart in June. These periods renew in us these different devotions.

Although there is a feast of the blessed sacrament, the entire year is not enough for our eucharistic veneration. If we wish, we can have the singular happiness of communicating every day. Let us look carefully into our heart where Jesus comes so often.

Do we find humility, patience, simplicity, love of God and neighbor, angelic purity—the marvelous lot of the little queen? If so, we are imitators of Therese. Does our divine visitor discover in us some resemblance to His beloved little spouse? Do we fervently compete with her in receiving the Eucharist?

If it is true that Communion is not a reward for virtue but a means of acquiring it, that the Church urges—by a generous and maternal gesture—her children to approach the holy table each day, let us not forget that she has dispensed no one from the required preparation and thanksgiving. Is it because Jesus gives himself so often that he is received with less devotion? Surely not. It would be embarrassing to acknowledge this.

Let us imitate the saint of Lisieux, naively ingenious at preparing her pure soul, awaiting the favor of her God. Let us combat routine commonplace and form our souls with deep respect. Let us ask ourselves, "Who is coming?"

Filled with admiration we can answer, "It is the Holy God, the living God, the plenitude of being, before whom the angels veil their faces repeating, 'holy, holy, holy is the Lord God of armies.' It is the same Christ whose sandal John the Baptist, precursor and forerunner of holiness, did not consider himself worthy to untie."

To whom does this divine Host come? To the worst of sinners, to a poor sinful nothing.

Let us make humble acknowledgement to God and with contrite heart recite the confiteor. And when the priest raises the Host, saying, "Behold the Lamb of God," let us ardently long for this amiable Lamb, this divine flake of whiteness, which for a moment trembles above the ciborium while waiting to be dissolved and lost in the furnace of our hearts.

Let us leap with joy because the bridegroom is drawing near and "the Morning Star rises at last in our hearts."[17]

COLLOQUY: With the Blessed Sacrament

> My Heaven is concealed in the little host
> Where Jesus, my Spouse, by love is hidden;
> I draw from this hearth the life I boast
> And there day and night, my sweet Spouse listens.
> What happiness, when with a tender kiss
> You come, my Spouse, to transform me to Thee;
> This union of love, this rapturous bliss—
> This is Heaven for me!
>
> *St. Therese of the Child Jesus*

Notes

1. In his discourse at the time of the promulgation of the decree concerning the heroic virtues of the servant of God.

2. "Come, spouse of Christ." Ancient liturgy in the consecration of virgins.

3. Is. 53:3.

4. This is shortly after the death of Therese. The negative impression of the body of Jesus was discovered on the positive plate of the photograph. Inspired by this picture, Celine Martin painted a negative likeness of Christ to which Pius X attached many indulgences expressing the desire "that this holy image finds its place in all Christian families."

5. Mark 10:14.

6. It was not until St. Pius X issued his decree of 1910 promulgating the reception of first Holy Communion for children "as soon as they begin to have a certain sense of reason.

7. Amos 8:11.

8. Therese is evidently speaking of the highest degree of union which permits the weakness of the creature and the divine strength to exist together.

9. Deposition of Sr. Frances Therese (Leonie) at the process of the ordinary, p. 132.

10. Song of Songs, 8:8.

11. Prayer of St. Ignatius of Loyola.

12. This letter on the eucharistic doctrine so unerring, though forgotten at the time it was written, stirred the admiration of St. Pius X.

13. *Histoire d'une Ame,* Ch. 5, p. 80.

14. Prov. 9:5.

15. *Biographie de Soeur Therese de l'Enfant Jesus,* Monsignor Laveille, p. 265.

16. *Imitation,* 4, 1, Ch. 3, 2.

17. II Peter 1:19.

Chapter Nine
Her Devotion to the Blessed Mother

O Immaculate Virgin! O thou the sweet Star
Which radiates Jesus and unites me to Him!
O Mother, allow me to hide under your veil
Just for today!

St. Therese of the Child Jesus

"Child of Mary, Child of paradise," says an old proverb. While truly predestined, the little saint of Lisieux maintained the sweetest and most filial relations with our Lady.

The maternal solicitude of Mary for Therese

Most important was the grace she obtained from being born into a Christian household where Marian devotion was practiced.

The month of Mary was a family event. Madame Martin wanted the altar of the Blessed Virgin faultlessly decorated.

"Mama is too hard to please, harder to please than the Blessed Virgin!" wrote the eldest daughter to Pauline, then a boarder at the Visitation. "She has to have hawthorne branches which reach to the ceiling, and the walls adorned with greenery."

Imagine the newfound wonder which shone in the eyes of the Benjamin before such an exhibition. Each morning her enthusiasm knew no bounds.

"She comes leaping with joy to say her prayers to the Blessed Virgin," announced Marie. "You ought to see how impish and foxy she is! yet, I marvel at her—she's the limit! Everyone in the whole house smothers her with kisses."

In the evening, there were other devotions. This time there were lights. Two lighted candles, burning down in a minute, made up the ceremony. Victoria recited the memorare quickly before the candles went out.

The madonna, for which little Therese put herself to so much trouble, was a reproduction of the original work done in silver by Bouchardon for the Church of St. Sulpice in Paris. A pious lady, surnamed in Alencon The Saint, had given it as a gift to Monsieur Martin before his marriage. Twice, this statue became animated on behalf of Therese's mother.

Once Madame Martin had just lost her little Helene, who died of consumption at the age of five and a half. The poor mother, recalling the one day a little lie had escaped those childish lips, wept at the feet of our Lady and said to her, "Oh! how I would like to know that my little Helene is not in purgatory."

A mysterious voice seemed to come from the statue, answering, "She is here at my side."

A few years later, the virgin granted Therese a pledge of her protection. The child was afflicted with a serious illness, the origin thought to be diabolically influenced.

Terrifying visions, incoherent words, lethargies lasting for hours, was the state little Therese was in.

At times in her delirium, she was tempted to jump over her bed railing and plunge into space. It was necessary to restrain her. One Sunday during High Mass, Leonie, having left her for a moment, returned to find her poor little sister stretched out on the floor between the bed and the wall. She did not recognize anyone and was striking her head violently against the side of the bed.

Dr. Notta, witness to these strange scenes and a conscientious practitioner, declared without hesitation. "Science is powerless in face of these phenomena; there is nothing that can be done."[1]

Nevertheless, Therese declares in her autobiography that even during the worst part of her illness she never lost consciousness, nor did she lose her reason. She avowed, that she felt as if she were under the influence of an evil spirit which—for reasons which we shall understand shortly—wanted to make an attempt on her life.

In view of such a hopeless case, Monsieur Martin turned to the queen of heaven. He had a novena of Masses said in the Church of Our Lady of Victories to obtain the cure which earthly doctors declared impossible.

"How touched I was at seeing his faith and his love," reported the saint. "How I would have liked to have gotten up and tell him I was cured! Alas! my desires could not perform a miracle, but Our Lady of Victories was capable of it and she did it entirely."

One Sunday during the novena, her sisters thought the poor sufferer's last hour had come.

Bewildered, they knelt and cried before the madonna. Then the eldest sister began to implore "with the fervor of a mother who simply had to have the life of her child." This cry forced the gates of heaven open.

"No longer finding any help on earth and almost dying with grief," Therese said, "I, too, turned to my heavenly Mother and begged her with all my heart to have pity on me."

"All of a sudden, the statue became animated! The Virgin Mary became beautiful so beautiful that I could never find words to describe that heavenly beauty; her face radiated kindness, an inexpressible tenderness; but what penetrated me to the depth of my soul was her charming smile!"

At this moment, the troubles of the little orphan vanished, tears of happiness rising in her eyes, silently rolling down her cheeks. Then Therese recognized her sister. She was cured.

"This vision lasted four to five minutes," reported Marie. "During this time Therese's face was radiant and as though in an ecstasy. Then her glance came to rest on me tenderly. From that time on, there no longer appeared any trace of her illness. The next day, she took up her ordinary way of life."[2]

At Carmel, the news of this marvel produced general excitement. The account, so simply and truthfully told by the child, was magnified, altered by the nuns, each one according to her own imagination.

Therese believed that she was the cause of these incorrect versions and experienced confusion until four years later. In the Church of Our Lady of Victories, our Lady, after consoling her soul, seemed to have let her understand the character of the apparition and the recovery.

One can imagine that the young girl, owing her life to our lady, did not neglect on any future occasion to show her gratitude.

Each year she regularly assisted the devotions for the month of Mary. During a holiday in the country with the Martin family at Deauville, she went to church for this purpose despite the distance, the stormy weather, and the weariness which at times resulted from the family's daily excursions.

On the day of her first communion, Therese was chosen to recite Consecration to the Blessed Virgin.

Soon this act of offering no longer satisfied her. She dreamed of becoming a child of Mary.

Mother St. Placid,[3] directress of the boarding school at the abbey, reflected, "We will not be sorry to have her name on our lists."

Indeed, the saintly child more than fulfilled what she had promised. One boarder, the future Sr. St. John the Evangelist, admired this gentle candidate who worked vigorously in silence and went to pray in the quiet of the chapel after finishing the lesson in her workbook.

On May 31, 1887, little Therese was officially enrolled among the children of Mary. After that she only aspired to become a Carmelite, to hide under the virginal mantle of her who takes first place in Carmel as its ornament and flower.

When one of her companions received the habit, St. Therese of the Child Jesus wrote these lines.

As a little lamb that is far from the fold,
Ignorant of danger, I frolic and play;
But O Queen of the heavens, my Shepherdess bold,
Your invisible hand bids my wantoness stay.
And so while I play on the cliff's very edge
You show me the summit of Carmel's delights
I then understand the troth that I pledge
Which urges me fly to the heavenly heights.

Her entrance into Carmel had been set for the feast of the annunciation but was delayed to April 9 because it was Lent.

"The Nativity of Mary! What a beautiful feast on which to become espoused to Jesus!" wrote the enthusiastic nun. "It was the little Virgin of the Nativity who presented her little flower to the little Jesus. On that day everything was little except the graces I received."

At day's end, Therese joyfully placed the crown of her ephemeral royalty at the feet of the madonna.

"I felt that time would not take away my happiness," she said.

Indeed, is not the mediatrix of grace the guardian and dispenser of lasting joy?

Therese, who entrusted to Mary her fragile crown of roses, was also convinced that her good mother would hold it in reserve and convert it into a dazzling crown of glory.

The filial tenderness of Therese for Mary

In her relations with the queen of heaven, Therese did not force herself into detailed ceremonies of etiquette. With marvelous foresight, she understood that the greatest queens are only simple women in the eyes of their children. So she placed herself in the arms of Mary with a cry of tenderness. "Mother!"

Reflecting, she said, "Do you know, my dear Mother, that I am happier than you are? I have you for Mother, and you do not have like me a Blessed Virgin to love! . . .

"It is true that you are the Mother of Jesus, but you have given Him to me; and He, on the cross, has entrusted you to us as our Mother; and so we are richer than you are! ...

"In your humility, you used to want to become the servant of the Mother of God; and I, spoiled as I am, I have the privilege of being your child!"

Then there was the exchange of confidences.

"I like to hide my troubles from God," she confessed, "because with Him I want everything to look rosy. But I tell the Blessed Virgin everything."[4]

Our Lord was not jealous at seeing himself excluded from these little domestic plots. Did He not know that his Mother and Therese conspired together only for his happiness?

Fearing that the holy and tender virgin would pity and comfort her with spiritual aridity she courageously repeated,

in face of these phenomena; there is nothing that can be done."[1]

Nevertheless, Therese declares in her autobiography that even during the worst part of her illness she never lost consciousness, nor did she lose her reason. She avowed, that she felt as if she were under the influence of an evil spirit which—for reasons which we shall understand shortly—wanted to make an attempt on her life.

In view of such a hopeless case, Monsieur Martin turned to the queen of heaven. He had a novena of Masses said in the Church of Our Lady of Victories to obtain the cure which earthly doctors declared impossible.

"How touched I was at seeing his faith and his love," reported the saint. "How I would have liked to have gotten up and tell him I was cured! Alas! my desires could not perform a miracle, but Our Lady of Victories was capable of it and she did it entirely."

One Sunday during the novena, her sisters thought the poor sufferer's last hour had come.

Bewildered, they knelt and cried before the madonna. Then the eldest sister began to implore "with the fervor of a mother who simply had to have the life of her child." This cry forced the gates of heaven open.

"No longer finding any help on earth and almost dying with grief," Therese said, "I, too, turned to my heavenly Mother and begged her with all my heart to have pity on me."

"All of a sudden, the statue became animated! The Virgin Mary became beautiful, so beautiful that I could never find words to describe that heavenly beauty; her face radiated kindness, an inexpressible tenderness; but what penetrated me to the depth of my soul was her charming smile!"

At this moment, the troubles of the little orphan vanished, tears of happiness rising in her eyes, silently rolling down her cheeks. Then Therese recognized her sister. She was cured.

"This vision lasted four to five minutes," reported Marie. "During this time Therese's face was radiant and as though in an ecstasy. Then her glance came to rest on me tenderly. From that time on, there no longer appeared any trace of her illness. The next day, she took up her ordinary way of life."[2]

At Carmel, the news of this marvel produced general excitement. The account, so simply and truthfully told by the child, was magnified, altered by the nuns, each one according to her own imagination.

Therese believed that she was the cause of these incorrect versions and experienced confusion until four years later. In the Church of Our Lady of Victories, our Lady, after consoling her soul, seemed to have let her understand the character of the apparition and the recovery.

One can imagine that the young girl, owing her life to our Lady, did not neglect on any future occasion to show her gratitude.

Each year she regularly assisted at the devotions for the month of Mary. During a holiday in the country with the Martin family at Deauville, she went to church for this purpose despite the distance, the stormy weather, and the weariness which at times resulted from the family's daily excursions.

On the day of her first communion, Therese was chosen to recite Consecration to the Blessed Virgin.

Soon this act of offering no longer satisfied her. She dreamed of becoming a child of Mary.

Mother St. Placid,[3] directress of the boarding school at the abbey, reflected, "We will not be sorry to have her name on our lists."

Indeed, the saintly child more than fulfilled what she had promised. One boarder, the future Sr. St. John the Evangelist, admired this gentle candidate who worked vigorously in silence and went to pray in the quiet of the chapel after finishing the lesson in her workbook.

On May 31, 1887, little Therese was officially enrolled among the children of Mary. After that she only aspired to become a Carmelite, to hide under the virginal mantle of her who takes first place in Carmel as its ornament and flower.

When one of her companions received the habit, St. Therese of the Child Jesus wrote these lines.

> All that He has given to me, Jesus can reclaim;
> Tell Him never to put Himself out for me!
> He can hide Himself; I'm willing to wait for Him
> Until the light dawns and faith is no more.

It is reasonable that a soul, accustomed to intimacy with Mary, should sometimes be disconcerted by sermons which speak exclusively on the prerogatives of the Mother of God.

"The holy Virgin would rather be imitated than admired," Therese said. "They make her appear inaccessible when they ought rather to show how she can be imitated. She is more Mother than queen. Her life was so simple!"

The novices whom she directed were astonished at this insight.

"This is my secret," she told them. "I never counsel you without calling upon the Blessed Virgin; I ask her to inspire me to know what must make you better; and as for myself, I am often surprised at the things which I teach you."

When one of the novices had some painful acknowledgement to make, she would lead her before the madonna who had smiled on her, saying, "You are not going to tell me, but the Blessed Virgin, about this thing which is costing you so much."

The servant of God had called our Lady the amiable queen of her virginal flock. So when a novice needed encouragement, she wrote to her in the name of that heavenly mistress.

It was on the inspiration of Therese that Sr. Genevieve of the Holy Face painted a portrait of the virgin mother. She perfected its meaning by adding a bit of poetry entitled "Heavenly Dew of Virginal Milk."

Her filial confidence in the intercession of "the all-powerful supplicant," as St. Bernard called her, was resolute.

"When we call upon the saints," she explained, "they tarry a little; they feel that they must present their request; but when we ask a favor of the Blessed Virgin, we receive immediate help . . . have you not noticed that? Try it and you will see!"

Rarely did Therese ask favors for herself. She loved God too much "to disturb and inconvenience Him for such a little thing." She also preferred to offer her suffocating and coughing spells in silence rather than contradict the divine plan by asking for their suppression. One evening Mother Mary of Gonzaga commanded her to make this request.

Afterwards Therese confided fearfully, "I have already asked the Blessed Virgin for that. . . . She . . . puts all my little desires in order; she expresses them or she doesn't express them; it is up to her to deal with it so as not to force God to hear me."

Once, when Mother Agnes of Jesus visited her, she observed that Therese seemed to have less suffering.

"Oh! just as much," she said. "I have a great deal of suffering! but the Blessed Virgin is the one to whom I complain."

Another time when she was misunderstood she confided, "The Blessed Virgin did well to keep all things in her heart."

The Virgin Mary—blessed among all women, yet more tried than any—taught Therese the value of suffering. These lines express her thought on this matter:

> Since the King of Heaven has willed that His Mother
>   Should submit in darkness to anguish of heart,
> Is it not then a blessing on earth to suffer?
>   Yes, since joy is the treasure sweet suffering imparts.

Her strength ebbing, St. Therese of the Child Jesus confided to a young sister, "I still have something to do before I die. I have always wanted to express in song all that I think of the Blessed Virgin."

Then she composed her Nunc Dimittis.

> I'd like to tell you, Mother, why I love you,
>   And why your name so sweet beguiles my heart,
> Any why your grandeur, majesty, and grace, too,
>   Does not alarm nor take me with a start...

Then she recalled the episodes in the life of her heavenly mother, drawing pleasant and wise lessons from them.

The last lines her unsteady hand wrote were full of veneration for her beloved mother.

"Mary," she said, "if you were Therese, and I were Mary, I would wish to be Therese so that you might be Queen of Heaven."

Pledging her filial love, the holy Carmelite wove, with feeble fingers, two simple wreaths of cornflowers. One was placed at the feet of the "Virgin of the Smile," the other in her hand.

Referring to this last wreath, a religious said to her, "You undoubtedly think this one here is being reserved for you?"

Therese answered, "Oh, no! the Blessed Virgin will do what she wants with it. What I give to her is for her pleasure."

Indeed, the Blessed Virgin did with it what she wanted. To-day, pilgrims can admire the faded but glorious wreaths in the relic room at Carmel.

But let us get back to our narrative.

Since the state of the sick nun was aggravated, the community began on June 5, 1897, to make a fervent novena to our Lady of victories. They hoped that the madonna would once again set her languishing little flower erect on its stalk. But Therese "had accomplished in a short time"[5] her task here below. She was ripe for heaven, and the queen of angels was already ready to pluck her.

Entering the infirmary, which would become her vestibule to heaven, Therese's glance showed inexpressible radiance toward the virgin of bouchardon.

"What do you see?" asked Sr. Marie of the Sacred Heart, who had been witness to her former ecstasy.

"Ah! the Blessed Virgin has never seemed so beautiful to me! but today, it is only the statue . . . before, you know very well it was not the statue!"

She said to her infirmary attendant, "Pray much to the Blessed Virgin for me, because if you were sick I would pray very much for you. When it is for oneself, one does not dare."

She believed herself a burden to those who cared for her. And said to the Madonna lovingly, "Good Blessed Virgin, what gives me a longing to die is that I make the infirmarian so tired and I am giving trouble to my Sisters in being so sick. Yes, I want so much to die!"

But her sisters were far from considering her departure a relief to them. Rather they dreaded the cruel separation.

"Outwardly, at least, death is sad!" sighed Mother Agnes of Jesus. "I will be so sorry to watch you die!"

Therese answered very tenderly, "The Blessed Virgin bravely held the lifeless body of her Jesus all disfigured and covered with blood on her knees. I don't know how she did it . . . I suppose they are already asking you in this case what will become of you?"

On August 19, the day of her last Communion, she felt ill during the recitation of the miserere.

"Perhaps I am losing my head," she said. "If only you knew

what I am going through! That night I was completely worn out, and I implored the Blessed Virgin to take my head in her hands so that I would be able to bear it."

A few days later, when a recurrence of moral anguish was joined to the usual physical suffering, Therese turned toward the image of Mary. In a weary voice, she sang to her sweetly.

> When will it come, my Mother dear;
>   When will come that beautiful day
> When from this land of exile drear
>   I will fly forever away?

At last, after a long and painful probation, the saintly child arrived at the end of her pilgrimage here below.

On the evening of September 30, 1897, when the monastery clock sounded the angelus, the dying nun riveted a gaze on the Virgin of the Smile.

Undoubtedly she repeated in her heart this song which rose to her lips many times.

> You who smiled on me at the dawn of life,
> Come, smile on me now . . . Mother, it is evening;
> I no longer fear the brightness of your heavenly glory.
> With you I have suffered; and I wish now
> To kneel at your feet, O virgin, and say why I love you,
> And to repeat forever that I am your child!

Practical Application

After enumerating the different practices of devotion toward the Blessed Virgin, Saint Grignon de Montfort added this important revelation. "The Most High has taught me a secret. I confide it to you through the Holy Spirit. . . . It is necessary to give oneself completely, in the capacity of a slave, to Jesus through Mary and to do all things through her, with her and in her."

Let us consider, too, the reasoning of St. Bernard.

"If all the graces come to us through the intercession of Mary," he said, "is it not fitting that grace returns to its author through the same channel?"

And is it not justifiable to consecrate ourselves to our Lady, going through her to Jesus since he came to us through her?

The advantages of a soul having the royalty of Mary are immeasurable. She tills this spiritual land as her own domain, bringing forth all the virtues. But since Mary is the fruitful virgin, she excels in bringing to birth and nurturing her son Jesus in a spiritual manner. This is her fruit and masterpiece, we learn from St. de Montfort.

Although St. Therese of the Child Jesus did not strictly follow the method which this servant of Mary indicates, she certainly possessed its spirit.

She lived intimately in a filial union with the queen of heaven, one of the main causes which contributed to her sanctity.

The heavenly mother of Therese is our mother also. Let us, too, confide to her with abandon, and everything will go well.

"Mary has a refined way about her," wrote a Franciscan author. 'Since she has, like all mothers, a characteristic mark of distinction: She likes to hear it said of her child: 'Oh, the pretty little thing.' That is why the Blessed Virgin puts pretty clothes on us, washes us, combs us so well, and finally curls our hair ... and I picture to myself the sweet smile of Jesus when He sees this little child improving under the touch of His Mother."[6]

If the most amiable and loving of mothers is to treat us in this way, it is necessary for us to run to her with the simplicity of Therese and, like her, direct our entire life toward the realization of that filial motto, "Ad Jesum per Mariam! To Jesus through Mary."

COLLOQUY: With the Blessed Virgin.

During this sad exile, here below, O Mother mine,
I wish to live with you, to follow you each day;

O Virgin, with delight I think of you and find
The same deep love that's in your heart, o'er mine
holds sway.

St. Therese of the Child Jesus

Notes

1. Deposition of Mother Marie of the Sacred Heart.
2. *Summarium of 1919*, p. 416.
3. Benedictine religious at the Abbey of Notre Dame du Pre.
4. *Summarium of 1919*, p. 490.
5. Wis. 4:13.
6. Reverend Pie De Wachter in *Le Messager de St. Francois*.

Chapter Ten
Her Way of Spiritual Childhood

Jesus, filled with joy by the Holy Spirit,
said: "I bless You Father, Lord of Heaven
and earth, for hiding these things from the
learned and the clever and revealing them to
little ones.

Luke 10:21

Entering Carmel, Therese resolutely stood before the imposing mountain of perfection. She considered its snowy peak, its rugged sides. Thoughtfully, she asked herself, "What must I do to get up there?"

After looking conscientiously for a lift, she said, "What if Jesus lifted me up? That would be the most excellent way of getting there. But would He? Elevators carry only cumbersome packages and small children!

"Very well, why can't I become a little child again? It would be delightful and very timely. Has not St. John the Baptist declared: 'He must increase and I must decrease'[1] if I would be like Him?"

In the silence of her prayers, the nun thought over these things. Opening the book of the Gospels, she lovingly reread the passage in which Christ, having blessed and embraced a little child, singled it out to his apostles as the most likely candidate for celestial glory. Therese thought about this happy child. Suddenly, she understood her way. Our Lord wanted her to be

115

distinguished in humility, simplicity, poverty, and filial abandon—the natural and gracious lot of childhood.

She applied herself to the work and fashioned from these four
virtues the synthesis which made her a saint and a child.

Very little childen are necessarily humble

Because they are conscious of their weakness, their littleness,
their ignorance.

The servant of God—although strong, magnanimous, and
intelligent—placed herself in the same category. Instead of appearing lofty and brave, she placed herself at their mercy.

A novice undergoing a trial said to her, "This time I cannot
rise above this difficulty."

"Why do you want to rise?" answered St. Therese of the Child
Jesus. "That is fine for great souls who soar above the clouds; as
for us, we humbly shoulder the avalanche, and afterwards bask
under the rays of divine love."

She explained to the sister how one day at Les Buissonnets, a
discussion going on about the best way to get past a horse block-
ing the road, she simply disappeared between the shanks of the
animal without saying a word, uninterrupting discussion.

"That is what comes from keeping little," she concluded.

This is symbolic of her spiritual tactic. Did someone point out
something about her? She felt she deserved it ten times over.
Had she committed a small fault? She was not surprised. "Children often fall," she said, "but without hurting themselves very
much."

She immediately amended it with God, like children who
come to their mother stretching their arms toward her, saying,
"Kiss me, I won't do it again."

She even said, "It would be my privilege to do foolish little
things until my dying day without offending God if I am humble, if I remain little. Look at little children—they are constantly
breaking things, tearing things up, and falling all over them-

selves while still loving their parents very much and being loved by them in return."

How did she account for her powerlessness to practice virtue? She pictured herself a child trying vainly to mount the first step of the stairs. On top, the mother watches and when her little one does not succeed in making the climb, she picks it up and takes it where it wants to be.

"God will do the same for us if we are humble," Therese taught, adding, "The only way to make rapid progress in the way of love is always to remain very little; that's what I have done; so now I can sing with our father St. John of the Cross: 'In bringing myself so low, so low/I raise myself so high, so high/ That I can attain my end."

This declaration never made her proud. Rather, she discovered it to be the work of God in her.

"To be little," she declared, "is not to attribute to oneself the virtues which one practices in the belief that one is capable of anything at all, but rather to recognize that this virtue belongs to God and that He places it in the hands of His little child so that He may be served by it."

A novice sighed, saying, "Ah! when I think of all that I have to acquire yet!"

"Say, 'to lose,'" retorted the wise mistress. "On the contrary, it is necessary that your soul be empty in order for Jesus to fill it. You are travelling backwards: you want to climb a mountain and Our Lord is waiting for you at the bottom in the fertile valley of humility."

A few of her daughters impatient to obtain perfection, she said to them, "Sanctity does not consist in such and such a practice, but in a disposition of the heart which makes us humble and little in the hands of God, conscious of our weakness and confident even to boldness in His Fatherly goodness."

Little children are simple

In spiritual matters, Therese ran quickly like a child. She did not lose time examining her conscience or the past.

"The only thing is to love God," she said, "while looking at ourself but not examining our faults too closely."

Her cousin Marie Guerin pleaded unworthiness in face of the grace of her vocation.

With her pen, Therese cut this knot of objections.

"Marie, if you are nothing, are you forgetting that Jesus is all? You have only to lose your little nothingness in Him and no longer think about anything except this uniquely loveable All."

Although attentive to the presence of God, Therese avoided intense applications of the mind.

"It is undoubtedly good to be recollected," she said, "but calmly, because constraint does not glorify God. He knows well what noble sentiments of love we would like to shower upon Him, and He is satisfied with our desires. Is He not our Father, and are we not his little children?"

Therese had the optimism of little ones.

"I always see the bright side of things," she confided. "There are some who lay hold of everything to make trouble for themselves. It is just the opposite with me: if I experience nothing but suffering, if heaven is so black that I can see nothing clearly, very well! I make that my joy."

The servant of God was simple in her speech, in her manner of walking, in all her actions.

In the refectory, she imagined that she was invited by the holy family of Nazareth. Since she was not hard to please, she very simply ate everything.

Naively, she offered St. Joseph something highly seasoned. The Blessed Virgin benefited from warm portions. The best was for the little Jesus.

When dinner was plainly abominable, Therese said to herself, "Today, little girl, everything is for you!"

Finding that mortification and simplicity paid off, the fervent Carmelite seized upon these occasions eagerly without complicating her life.

"There were times," she confided, "when I thought of repugnant things during my meals in order to mortify myself; but later on, I found it simpler to offer to God what I found appetizing and at the same time to thank Him for it."

When she was told about someone who had excessive longings for mortification, she loudly praised the heroism that such action implies, adding, "But I could not be so weighed down in that way; I have practiced virtue on a totally different scale after the manner of Our Mother, St. Teresa: 'God is not at all taken up with a host of trifles as we imagine, and He wants nothing to weigh the soul down.'"

Therese believed that extraordinary penance was not meant for her nor for souls walking in her way.

Indeed, one cannot see little children laden with hairshirts, flogging themselves. Their innocence on the one hand, their weak constitution on the other, seem bound to exempt them from these excessive mortifications.

"If they were indispensible, Our Lord would have told us and we would impose them on ourselves wholeheartedly," observed St. Therese of the Child Jesus. "He teaches us, on the contrary that 'there are many mansions in my Father's house.'[2] If there is one for the Fathers of the desert, for the martyrs, and the penitents, there must also be one for little children. Our place is reserved there."

Besides, Monsignor Gay taught that spiritual childhood is more perfect than love for suffering.

"Nothing immolates man so much as being sincerely and peacefully little," he wrote. "The spirit of childhood slays pride more surely than the spirit of penance."

The same simplicity found in the little saint is also seen in her relations with superiors. Her soul was crystal clear—not one shadow, not one crease, not one subterfuge. Nothing but absolute loyalty.

In her subordinates, she would not permit quibbling.

"You are wrong to criticize this and that, to desire that everybody conform to your way of seeing things," she said to a novice.

"Since you want to be one of the little children, little children do not know what is best but find good in everything; let us imitate them."

She desired interior simplicity so much that she put her free will in the hands of Jesus.

"Oh! How I would like to be drawn by Our Lord," she wrote. "With what sweetness have I given over my will to Him."

The simplicity of her relations with God was astonishing.

"On all occasions, I act with Him like a child who thinks everything is lawful," she avowed.

Surprised by the fear with which the seraphim veil their faces from God, she outwardly disapproved of this attitude.

"They tell me that in heaven I will be among the Seraphim," she said. "If that is so, I would not imitate them. I would be very careful in covering myself with my wings ... for then, I would no longer see God, I would be afraid—and how would it be possible for me to lavish my caresses on Him and to receive His?"

One day she was shown a picture of Christ surrounded by many children.

"As for me, I am that little one who has climbed upon Jesus' knees, who raises her little head and embraces Him without fearing anything," she says. "The other one does not appeal to me as much; it holds itself in reserve like some great personage."

This childlike thinking, so familiar to the servant of God, was not devoid of energy. The tone of this note is significant.

"I am not surprised at the defeats of a little child," she wrote to a novice. "It forgets that because it is so brave and valiant it must do without rather childish consolations."

She sang a verse composed no doubt for the same soul.

> In You alone, O Jesus, I abide;
> Into Your arms I run and safely hide;
> I want to love You like a little child,
> I want to wrestle for You warlike-styled.
> And like a babe so full of tendernesses
> I want, O Lord, to load You with caresses;

> And in the field of my apostolate
> Like a soldier brave, I steel myself for combat.

As for her personal conduct, there was no childishness. Therese did not make her sickness an excuse for relaxation. To this end, one of her daughters brought her an amusing illustrated book. She refused it, saying, "How can you think that this book can interest me. I am too near eternity to want to be distracted with trifles."

In her eyes, the splendors of the century were emptiness. Mother Agnes of Jesus, trying to divert her, recounted the triumphal reception given by France to the czar of Russia in 1897.

"Ah," she said, "all this pomp does not dazzle me! Speak to me about God, the examples of the saints, and all truth like that."

Since Therese did not have, in the solitude of the cloister, the sight of earthly children, she applied herself faithfully to imitating the children of heaven. The white cohort of the holy innocents marched in her mind. Despite her age, she aspired to join them.

"The Holy Innocents are not children in heaven," she affirmed, "they are only indefinable beauties of childhood. They represent children because we need images in order to understand invisible things. Yes, I hope soon to join them!"

Passing time, she addressed them with a set of couplets.

> It is you whom the Lord has given to me
> As a model, O Innocents fair.
> I wish to mirror you faithfully,
> Little children, of virtue rare.
> Oh! deign to obtain the virtue of trust,
> And child-like candor, too;
> Your perfect abandon, your innocent love
> Ever charms my heart anew.

"My protectors in heaven and my special friends are those who have stolen it like the Holy Innocents and the good thief.

Great Saints earned it by their works; as for me, I want to imitate the thieves, I want to get it through strategy—a strategy of love which will open the gates of heaven to me and to poor sinners. The Holy Spirit encourages me, since He says in Proverbs: 'Impart ... knowledge and discretion to the young.'"[3]

This divine lesson in discretion taught Therese the delightful diplomacy of little children who love spontaneously.

Little children are poor

They possess nothing of their own. They depend on their parents for everything. Like them, little Therese expected everything from the divine, precisely because of her littleness:

"Even in the homes of the poor, as long as the child is little, he is given everything necessary," she said, "but as soon as he grows up, his father tells him: 'work now, you can provide for yourself.'"

Therese considered herself incapable of earning a living and resolved never to grow up so as to remain indefinitely under the care of a guardian.

"I remained ever little," she confided, "having no other occupation than to pluck flowers of love and sacrifice and offer them to God."

That was the strategy which the lovable saint used. She took care not to hoard treasures, because she intended to appear before the sovereign judge with empty hands:

"I do not know how to save money," she said; "I immediately spend it to buy souls."

Was this a lack of wisdom on her part? By no means. The saint omitted calculating with God, knowing that he would be more eager to take her interests to heart. She was persuaded that the divine measure would always be greater and more than hers. And she excused herself from all censure, like little children who understand only what is necessary when it comes to arithmetic for the sake of being royally spoiled.

The servant of God was not ignorant of the fact that little children traveled free of charge, or at least at the expense of those who accompanied them. Likewise, in expectation of her great departure, she wrote her sister in the Visitation order, "All my efforts are directed at becoming a very little child . . . who has no preparations to make; Jesus Himself must pay the full expense of the trip and the price of entrance into heaven."

Not content with traveling free, little children are happy despite their poverty, because of their boundless trust.

Materially, they possess nothing. Their whole little fortune lies in their heart. With the small change of affection, they capitalize on this tenderness to bear fruit which yields a hundredfold.

Therese grasped the secret of these little ones, striving a thousand ways to prove her filial love for the all-powerful. So the little child of God, though personally without resources,[4] dispensed spiritual riches to souls with the liberality of a wealthy person. She gave out freely the infinite treasures of the Heavenly Father, the most magnanimous and loving of bankers.

Blessed are the poor in spirit who are enriched by the munificence of God himself!

Little children abandon themselves

Blindly to their parents. Therese was like them. "God wants me to abandon myself as a very little child who is not disturbed by what happens to it," she confided to Mother Agnes of Jesus.

She faithfully followed this divine inspiration. When she had to make a choice between two alternatives, death or transfer to Hanoi, her serenity was not disturbed.

"I am quite abandoned," she said, "to live or to die, or to recover my health in order to go to China if that's what God wants," adding, "I desire neither life nor death; if the Lord would offer me a choice, I would choose neither. I want only what He wants. Whatever He does I love."[5]

Regarding her death, her abandonment remained the same.

"If you find me dead in the morning, do not be sad," she charged her sisters. "It is just that God will have come quite simply to get me. No doubt it is a great grace to receive the sacraments, but when God does not permit it, it is a blessing just the same . . . everything is a grace."

St. Therese of the Child Jesus had painted little angels in fresco in the interior oratory of Carmel.

She said one day, pointing to an angel sleeping with its elbows leaning against the tabernacle, "I am that little angel; it is sleeping but its heart watches."[6]

She indicated by this that her peaceful abandon had nothing in common with the heresy of quietism, since it took nothing from her vigilance.

The servant of God, in her prudence, feared this danger. "Be very careful," she cautioned a religious who intended to explain the way of spiritual childhood. "Because the Little Way wrongly understood can be taken for quietism or illuminism in the manner of Madame Guyon. It is not a way of rest however, oh! quite the contrary!"

Not letting her hope wither under the pretext of abandonment, Therese ardently desired heaven because she had a presentiment of the ineffable privileges reserved for little ones.

"I figure that the chosen places which Jesus refused to the sons of Zebedee, and who nevertheless became apostles and martyrs, will become the lot of children," she said. "Does not David predict this when he says: 'Benjamin, the youngest, is leading them'?"[7]

Our Lord had not been explicit on this subject, because, to the ambitious James and John, he could make no other answer than this. "As for seats at my right hand or my left, these are not mine to grant; they belong to those to whom they have been allotted."[8]

Did Christ not evoke at this instant, in his omniscient thought, the two profiles of the two privileged beings who had so ideally surrounded his infancy—his holy mother and his foster father. Mystery of predestination not up to us poor mortals to fathom!

Be that as it may, Therese seems to have had a clear idea of the boldness of her childlike hopes. She excused herself amiably in her autobiography by saying, "My excuse is my title of child. Little children do not reflect on their manner of speaking. . . . Nevertheless, if their parents come into an inheritance, they do not hesitate to satisfy the desires of the little ones whom they cherish more than themselves. In order to please them, they do foolish things; they even go so far as to descend to weakness."

Such was the immense confidence of Therese, this loving little child of God. Is it any wonder that from the time she abandoned herself to Him she sang sweetly to him until the evening of her life?

My heaven is to feel the likeness within
    Of the God Who breathed life in me all undefiled;
My heaven is to remain in His Presence anon
    To call Him my Father and to be His child;
I'm clasped in His arms; the storm holds no fear . . .
    For total abandon is the law which sets free!
To rest on His heart, see His face e'er so near
    That is heaven for me!

Practical Application

A few weeks before her death, Therese said to Mother Agnes of Jesus in an inspired voice, "I feel that my mission is going to begin, my mission to give to souls my Little Way."

"What little way do you want to teach them?" asked her sister.

"Mother, it is the Way of Spiritual Childhood, the way of confidence and total abandonment. I want to point out to souls the ways which to me are so perfectly successful: to throw to Jesus the flowers of little sacrifices, to win Him by caresses. That is how I won Him, and it is for that that I shall be well remembered."

This "little way," authorized by the one who confirmed it by

miracles, has won innumerable followers even among intellectuals. It seems that the Lord realized in Therese this passage from Holy Scripture, "The least shall become a thousand,
and a little one a most strong nation."[9]

"We who are called 'scholars,'" wrote a superior of the order,
"we may teach to the world a very wise theology, one which the
faithful have not the time to listen to. And the Lord had pity on
this crowd. He took a child, Therese, and placed her in the midst
of His apostles. And this child revealed to them such simple and
delightful truths that the scholars suffered their ignorance to be
exposed and set about following the child in order to teach her
doctrine to the people."[10]

A bulletin put out at the University of Paris read, "Little Sister,
lead us in this way of spiritual childhood which is your own way;
and disconcerting as it may be for our pride and our restlessness,
show that it is the surest and most direct way to God."

When the decree on the heroic virtue of the servant of God
was promulgated, His Holiness Benedict XV made a doctrinal
commentary which could be summarized in this way: spiritual
childhood is the secret of sanctity.

His successor, Pius XI, did not hesitate to declare, "It has
pleased God to make known to the whole world the perfect
practice of spiritual childhood in which Therese, simply and
innocently, revealed herself to be a master."

The way of spiritual childhood is not pious child's play—
leaving posterity unprovided for—but a method of perfection
whose efficacy has been affirmed by the most qualified here
below. If we are imitators of Therese, we should take up its
practice.

"But," mature persons will object, "is it not ridiculous for me
to play the part of a simple child?"

Granted, but that is not what St. Therese of the Child Jesus
asks of you. She was most certainly not in conflict with the great
apostle who recommended, "In what concerns malice, you can
be childlike, but mentally you must be adult."[11]

"If I had lived until I was eighty, I would still remain as little as I am now; I know it well," affirmed Therese. "Age is nothing in the eyes of God. It is possible to remain little even under the most formidable burdens and to extreme old age."

Pius IX, who certainly bore the most formidable burden which can be handed to another human being, agreed.

"My only ambition is to become a little child in the arms of God," he wrote.

May this statement be ours from now on. It is the surest way of pleasing the Lord. "It is enough to be little for that reason alone," we learn from the servant of God.

From that moment, what calm surrounds our souls! It as easy to rise as to descend. It is as simple to become gentle, humble, and little as it is to become heroic. And why? Because every being finds his full development in his normal situation. But nothing is more normal than acknowledging our littleness, our weakness, our frailty.

Let us then be little in our own eyes, not being deceived by our personal worth. Let us be friendly and sincere toward all, like little children who do not know prejudice and social pretense.

Little children are sometimes "unmanageable" because of their frankness. Let us imitate them with the reserve that charity and discretion demands. One must not say all that one thinks. One must rather think of what one is saying. This way, an upright and loyal soul is formed. It is said that God sees himself in his own clear gaze.

Let us, too, strive to become souls of light and wisdom, not only by our frankness but above all by the simple and supernatural character of our intentions. Let us direct them toward Jesus and his glory without tolerating in ourselves pompousness of pride or cowardice of human respect.

Let us profit by the following reflection that an old Carmelite made to Therese of the Child Jesus a short time after her entrance into Carmel.

"Little girl, your soul is extremely simple; but when you are perfect, you will become even more simple. The nearer one comes to God, the more simple she is."

These are profound words dictated by experience, and deserve to be meditated upon.

Finally—after living in humility, poverty, honesty, and simplicity—let us especially imitate their delightful abandon.

Consider a little child in the arms of its mother. No matter how dark the night, the dangers that surround it, it is never disquieted. It sleeps like one of the blessed on its mother's breast, ready to smile and embrace her when it wakes up.

Let us abandon ourselves with this filial tenderness into the arms of the living God. Let us be a credit to His paternal love. Has He not created the mother's heart. Has he not been more vigilant, more loving, and above all more powerful, than the most devoted of mothers? Let us show Him our tenderness with the holy familiarity of little Therese. We will thrill His heart. He will condescend us, and his all-powerful arms will become the spiritual lift which will raise us to the ethereal regions of perfection. Our Heavenly Father will accomplish in a flash what our puny self-will could not have realized in many years.

"God does not need years to accomplish His work of love in a soul," said Therese. "A single ray from His Heart can, in one moment, make His little flower blossom for eternity."

It is essential to obtain this ray. Where grown-ups, scholars, and the mighty fail, little ones, by the conquering charm of their love, triumph. Little children, praise the Lord!

COLLOQUY: With our Heavenly Father.

> In littleness my peace abounds
>   So that when I chance to fall
> Jesus takes me by the hand
>   And I rise quickly at His call.

St. Therese of the Child Jesus

Notes

1. John 3:30.
2. John 14:2.
3. Prov. 1:4.
4. At least, so she thought in her humility.
5. Personal notes cited in *L'Esprit de Ste. Therese de L'Enfant Jesus*, p. 157.
6. Song of Songs 5:2.
7. Ps. 68:27.
8. Mark, 10:40.
9. Is. 60:22.
10. Preface of *L'Histoire d'une Ame*, p. XXI.
11. I Cor. 14:20.

Chapter Eleven
Her Sufferings

Helpless, without light and in darkness,
I am being consumed by love.

St. John of the Cross

Nothing worthwhile can be accomplished without suffering, affliction, or trials permitted by God or effected by men.

Reading the lives of the saints, we are inspired to pious thoughts and generous resolutions. We must not be content, as in secular reading, with admiring them superficially. Rather, we must bear in mind that the price of their sanctity produces supernatural blessings.[1]

Moreover, if in our day St. Therese of the Child Jesus worked such marvelous transformation in souls, one can rightfully believe that this redemptive work was due to sufferings by which Therese made it fruitful.

At times the young Carmelite was accused of being "a little rosewater saint" who had never known sacrifice.

Those who went along with this opinion were only superficial readers. For it is not easy to perceive at first, among so many flowers, how the stem of her life was grafted to the tree of the cross. "O Crux Ave."[2]

Those who know the power of Therese with almighty God realize that there is no need to refute such a statement. First of all, let us consider the testimony of the servant of God herself who declared two months before her death, "I have suffered much here below. Could this be a falsehood simply because it was not evident to anyone most of the time?"

Knowing that the posthumous publication of her autobiography was intended, "she insisted that souls should be well aware that she had suffered much."

Her mental sufferings.

The first time the vibrant soul of Therese came to grips with reality was upon the death of her mother.[3]

It seems that her little daughter's playfulness and youthful gaiety had been buried with Madame Martin for ten years.

"Therese went through a long period of darkness," recalled Celine, the companion of her childhood. "She suffered at this period with continuous headaches; but her extreme sensitiveness was her greatest source of affliction which she endured without ever complaining."[4]

One of Therese's teachers at the abbey gave this striking picture of her.

"She habitually wore a thin, delicate smile which appeared as soon as her tears, which flowed too easily and frequently, were dried."[5]

Her mother's death, the departure of her two sisters for Carmel, the persistent scruples, and the taunts from classmates jealous of her academic success—these were her main trials.

To these facts are joined a subjective state of keen sensitivity which made her life a veritable little martyrdom until Christmas 1886.

A few months later, the measures she took to gain entrance into Carmel brought new disappointments. The answers of Leo XIII and Bishop Hugonin continued to be paternally evasive, that of her pastor[6] peremptorily negative. Despite himself, the pastor introduced the young aspirant to Carmel six months later.

We have already described the cordiality of her reception. For the poor heart of Therese which had been bruised by such cruel separations, it was nothing less than comforting.

One can suppose that the unction of grace would compensate for those tribulations. Nothing was further from the truth. From the beginning, she experienced complete dryness. Moreover, as we have already pointed out, she was severely treated by the prioress. Finally, other trials descended upon her which were even more acute, known only to God.

The young postulant who expected only suffering in religion was astonished by the least joy.

"Illusions!" she wrote. "God in his mercy, has preserved me from them. I have found religious life just what I thought it would be; no sacrifice surprises me; and my first days in Carmel were met with more thorns than roses. Yes, I must say, suffering held out its arms to me from the very beginning and I embraced it with love," adding, "For five years this is the path I trod, but I was the only one to know it. That was precisely the hidden blossom that I wanted to offer to Jesus, one whose perfume is exhaled only in heaven."

On the eve of her profession, during the night watch in choir usually so sweet for brides of Christ, the devil incited the novice to a fiendish temptation.

"He made me think that life in Carmel was never meant for me," she said, "that I was deceiving my superiors in advancing upon a way of life to which I was not called. The shadows became to dense that I understood only one thing: I had no vocation, and I must return to the world. . . . Oh! what agonies I suffered!"

Indeed, what could have been more painful than to be tortured by such uncertainty on the eve of a decision which would bind her for life? Open-heartedness and submission delivered her from this dilemma. She pronounced her vows the next day.

Her taking of the veil a few days later was, in the words of Therese, "all veiled in tears." Monsieur Martin was too ill to be there, and his poor little queen suffered cruelly in this newest trial.

Indeed, the health of this dearly beloved father caused his daughters grave concern. Two attacks of paralysis had already made them fear a cerebral disorder, and a third made them realize only too clearly these sad conjectures. On February 12, 1889, Monsieur Martin was taken to a nursing home where he stayed for three years.

One day, the poor invalid, watched constantly, got away and wandered about for three days before being found. His Carmelite daughters, powerless because of their enclosure, underwent the worst agonies.

Mother Therese of St. Genevieve, supernaturally enlightened, told them that he would be found the next day. And that is what happened.

When St. Therese of the Child Jesus had undergone trials before, she had surprised Mother Mary of the Angels by saying, "I'm suffering very much, but I can still suffer more," This time, however, she felt that she had reached her limit.

"Oh! I can no longer say that I am able to suffer more. Just as the sufferings of Jesus pierce the heart of His heavenly Mother so do our hearts feel deeply the wounds and humiliations of those whom we cherish on earth."

The servant of God, generous as she was, tried to rise above her feelings and see this painful trial in a supernatural light.

She recalled the prophetic vision she had at Les Buissonnets and Monsieur Martin's recent offering of himself as a victim, and she understood that this severe trial emanated from the divine hand of God.

This was enough to make her love Him. But she did not stop at that. She thoroughly examined the advantages of this cross which detached, humiliated, purified, and sanctified their souls, then exulted like the apostle "who rejoiced exceedingly in the midst of his tribulations."[7]

"What a privilege from Jesus," she wrote Celine. "How He must love us to send us such a great sorrow! . . . Eternity will not be long enough to bless Him for it. He loads us with favors as He does the greatest of saints. What then is His plan of love for our souls?" She added in her autobiography, "Our father's three years of martyrdom seem to me to be the kindest and the most fruitful of our lives; I would not exchange them for the most sublime ectasies."

After three sorrowful years, Monsieur Martin's paralysis had become generalized. Celine brought him back to Lisieux where he lived yet another three years.

During his illness, his cloistered daughters only saw him once. Upon leaving them, crying, he pointed heavenward, barely able to pronounce the phrase, "In heaven."

On July 29, 1894, God brought the calvary of his faithful servant to an end.

Henceforth, St. Therese of the Child Jesus, when praying in her Carmelite cell, could repeat more fervently than ever, "Our Father, Who art in Heaven."

Perhaps it will be said of her, "True, Therese was orphaned at an early age. But after all, her sisters stayed with her and she found the joys of family life in the midst of them."

This would be the wrong attitude, because Therese courageously shunned those affections and satisfactions which the rule of Carmel does not permit.

Knowing her death near, she bid her sisters, saying, "When I am gone, be very careful not to live a 'family life.' Watch that you don't exchange stories without permission of what takes place in the parlor, and do not seek this permission unless it is absolutely necessary."

She wrote in her autobiography, "It is a source of much suffering to live in community with one's sisters when they are determined not to give in to nature."

It is like brothers fighting alongside each other on a battlefield.

"They sustain each other," she acknowledged, "but to make up for it, does not the martyrdom of one become the martyrdom of all?"

She spoke from experience, because when it was a question of sending two of her sisters to the Carmel of Hanoi, Therese secretly shed tears.

"My heart was broken at the thought of the trials which awaited them; but I would not utter a single word to hold them back."

When Leonie entered the Visitation after a fruitless attempt with the Poor Clares, Therese rejoiced "that the little dove has finally entered the ark." She did not feel the least bitterness by this final separation. She wrote Sr. Frances Therese,[8] "There is no doubt that my joy is entirely spiritual because from now on I will never see you here below, and will never again hear your voice when I open my heart to you."

The entrance of Celine into the Lisieux Carmel brought pinpricks for the Martin sisters from certain religious who did not approve of the presence of four sisters and one cousin[9] in a monastery of twenty people.

If it had been a question of less perfect and less mortified souls, they would assuredly have been able to form a clique not wanting in influence. But the saint made it a rule of never seeking the company of her sisters at recreation. When they were ill in bed, she was not the first to visit them.

Outside the parlor, her reserve with them was such that after her death one of the Carmelites expressed to Sr. Marie of the Sacred Heart her astonishment that she had so rarely sought the company of her holy little sister.

"How could I get to her?" Marie answered. "I certainly wanted to, but she was so faithful to the Rule that she would not speak to me."[10]

However, with Mother Agnes of Jesus, her prioress for three years, and Celine, who became her novice, her relationships with them were more intimate.

But for five years before her sister became prioress, the servant of God did not communicate with her whatsoever, even though they worked together in the refectory.

"O little Mother," she confided afterwards, "how I suffered then! I was not able to open my heart to you and I thought that you no longer knew me!"

On the evening of the election of Sr. Agnes of Jesus, the heart of little Therese pounded with joy at the thought that from now on she could speak to her little mother with complete freedom, as she had formerly."[11]

In a spirit of mortification, she never abused it, though. After her term was over Mother Agnes of Jesus still came, with permission of the new prioress, but Therese would no longer permit the least confidence.

She would have had only to ask to obtain the necessary permission.

"But," she declared, "it is not necessary to give liberties which sweeten religious life to the point of making it less meritorious."[12]

When St. Therese of the Child Jesus became consumptive, when her soul was tormented by interior trials and her body racked by continuous fever, it would have been natural for her to seek comfort and support from her beloved sisters.

But the saint desired to be deprived of the sweetness of their presence and dreamed of dying for Jesus, abandoned on a distant shore.

"I wish to go to Hanoi," she confided. "Here I am loved, and this affection is very dear to me; that is why I dream of a monastery where I would be unknown, where I would suffer exile of heart."

To this degree of heroism, the soul of Therese, eager for suffering, was to be elevated.

Her physical sufferings

The more perfect a person, the more that person is apt to suffer. The servant of God was privileged soul with a sensitive heart and a frail body. This threefold gift made her particularly prone to suffering. Her physical sufferings were comparable to her spiritual and mental trials.

From entering Carmel, despite her age and childhood illness, she was ordered by Mother Mary of Gonzaga to follow the rule except for fasting.

Her companions, would at times seek dispensation for her from the night office or from early arising. But the prioress invariably answered, "Dispensations are not made for a soul of such calibre; leave her alone—God will support her. Besides if she is ill, she should say so."

The fervent novice practiced the advice of the reformer of Carmel who persuaded her daughters "to go to the limits of their strength before complaining."[13]

Still the energetic little nun, plagued with dizziness and neuralgia, continued to attend matins.

"I can still walk," she told herself. "So! I must perform my duty."

Like an old soldier, always at her post, she accomplished heroic acts simply.

Clothed with the habit, she was given a heavy material. She wore it joyfully without the least hint of fatigue.

When she perspired in summer, or suffered from winter cold, she preferred not to wipe her face or rub her hands "in the hopes that God would not see it."

"It is painful enough that Our Lord must leave us on this earth to complete our probation without our constantly coming to Him to tell Him we are ill."[14]

In this way the saint developed the art of suffering in silence.

When one of her companions pricked Therese's shoulder while fastening the pin of her scapular, the servant of God did not utter a single complaint. Asked later how long she had endured this acute pain, without adjusting the pin, she answered simply, "For several hours. I went to the wine cellar to refill the bottles and I brought them back in baskets. I was so happy; but finally I was afraid of not being obedient since our Mother knew nothing about it."[15]

During the young Carmelite's first year in the monastery, cider was drunk in the refectory. She sat near an old sister who shared the same bottle. This religious, afflicted with an illness which made her thirsty, did not take into account that invariably she would leave only the dregs in the decanter for her neighbor. Considerately, Therese did not take water for fear of humiliating the sister, so depriving herself almost entirely of drink.[16]

That she habitually endured such painful privation revealed a spirit of extraordinary mortification.

Therese's frail stomach did not adjust easily to the frugal fare of Carmel. Certain food made her sick, but she hid it so well that no one suspected.[17]

Since the little sister never complained, she was thought exceptionally robust. So the sisters in the kitchen invariably served her leftovers. Often her meal would be pieces of fried fish, dry as a board, since they had been reheated so often.

Finally, after seven years, God put a stop to this. One deeply distressed sister said to the prioress, "Mother, I must warn you that the health of that poor Sr. Therese of the Child Jesus is being ruined."[18]

Nevertheless, in the eyes of Therese, these mortifications were a small matter.

"I was attracted to penance," reads her manuscript, "but I could find nothing to satisfy it." Let us analyse this "nothing" and be surprised to find how much weight it carried.

The diet we will describe was not a gourmet menu.

In Carmel, there is perpetual abstinence. The fast prescribed by the rule is six months out of the year not counting the regular fast days of the Church, every Wednesday and numerous vigils. This fast only allows one meal about noon and a light meal in the evening. This makes the morning's toilsome work particularly laborious.

Carmelites are expected to remain in the solitude of their

rooms for a considerable part of the day and are encouraged to keep silence except during recreation hours. They chant or recite the canonical hours and spend considerable time in private prayer or meditation. The tunic of these religious was of rough serge—too hot in summer, too cold in winter.

For certain temperaments, deprivation of sleep is great mortification. Going to bed at eleven and rising at five caused the delicate Therese to be overcome at times with weariness in choir. Still, she accused herself of lacking fervor!

What she suffered from most during the long, rainy Normandy winters was lack of heat.

During cold spells, the servant of God, after being chilled the whole day, would go to the community room after matins to warm herself for a few minutes. But to get to this room, she had to walk the length of the cloister in the open air, so the little warmth that she obtained soon vanished.

When she lay on her straw mattress and pulled the two poor coverlets over her, she found only relative relief. At times, she trembled through the night without sleeping.

The mistress of novices would have soon remedied this situation had she been informed, but Therese accepted this severe mortification without complaining. Only on her deathbed did she reveal it.

"What I have suffered most from physically during my religious life was the cold; I almost died from it."[19]

Her hands swollen and cracked with chilblains, still she took no notice of it.[20] She exposed herself piteously to the wind, even washing her linens outside in icy water instead of in the warm laundry.

For a long time, on her chest Therese wore a little cross with iron hooks which sank into her flesh. Only because she developed an infection did she give up this instrument of penance.[21]

For those who stride to perfection through keeping their holy rule, there are a number of other restrictions which help make religious life what St. Therese called, "a martrydom of pin pricks."

The remarkable austerites mentioned above are not temporary, only performed when the body and soul are ready. No, this cross is carried with all changes in health—as expressed in the vow formula—"And this until death."

Considered humanly[22] is not such an existence an anticipated death? Is it not simpler to shed one's blood on the battle field, to give one's life all at once with a single blow, than to file it down hour by hour?

Nevertheless, we have seen that for St. Therese of the Child Jesus the perfect observance of the austere rule was nothing.

Then what did she want in her thirst for sacrifice? To imitate, to surpass, the frightening penances of the desert fathers? Yes, this was—implicitly, at least—her desire.

But the Holy Spirit made her understand that this zeal was untimely, that it was not in keeping with the way of childhood, and that superfluous mortification was not for her. She then renounced them.

Instructed in this school of divine wisdom, she recommended at the end of her life "moderation in penances . . . because often nature rather than virtue enters into it."

She said to Mother Agnes of Jesus, "There is in the life of Blessed Henry Suso a passage which struck me relative to corporal penances. He had performed frightful ones which ruined his health when an angel appeared to him and told him to stop, adding: 'You have still only fought like a simple soldier; now I am going to dub you a knight.' And it was given to the Saint to understand the superiority of spiritual combat over mortifications of the flesh.

"Well, Mother," concluded Therese, "God does not want me to be like a simple soldier; I have suddenly been knighted and I am setting out on a war against myself in the spiritual realm by abnegation, little hidden sacrifices. I have found peace and humility in this dark combat where nature has taken nothing."[23]

To these acts of abnegation she joined other mortifications not harmful to her health. One fast day, the mother prioress imposing a remedy upon her, she was surprised by a seasoning too sweet to her taste.

When one of her companions once saw her slowly drink a loathsome medicine, she said, "Hurry up! drink it down in one gulp!"

"Oh, no," Therese replied, "can I not take advantage of the few occasions that come my way to mortify myself a little since I am forbidden to look for big things?"[24]

The time had come for God to fully satisfy the immense desires for suffering which consumed the saint.

On the night of Holy Thursday 1896, returning to her room after midnight, she had a pulmonary hemorrhage. The next day at dawn she recounted the incident to her prioress, who, misled by the energy and gaiety of Therese, did not take the whole thing seriously. Instead of tending to her illness immediately, she permitted her to take part in the austerities customary to Carmel on Good Friday—fasting on bread and water, spending hours kneeling in prayer, praying with one's arms in the form of a cross, taking the discipline, and so on.

In between the long liturgical offices, she was allowed to wash the monastery windows.

Despite her courage, Therese's strength gave way under this exhausting work. A novice, alarmed by her livid complexion, tearfully begged that she might be allowed to ask for some help.

But her mistress refused, "saying that she was well able to stand slight fatigue on this day when Jesus had suffered so much for her."[25]

The baneful consequence of this heroism, more to be admired than imitated, is easy to see. The next night, the spitting of blood again occurred. Mother Mary of Gonzaga still did not think there was anything to worry about. Therese was left unattended for several weeks until a stubborn cough attracted the attention of the prioress.

Dr. Corniere, the community's physician, and Dr. LaNeele, a cousin of the invalid through marriage, were consulted and prescribed a series of vigorous treatments—general massages, plasters, cuppings, lancings—all the known methods of the day. St. Therese of the Child Jesus endured with equanimity.

Her condition remained the same for some months, but in November 1896 it worsened. This time a high, continuous fever and persistent digestive disorders rapidly consumed the organism already so wasted away.

Despite these alarming symptoms, Mother Mary of Gonzaga allowed her to follow the community exercises.

In the dead of winter, the little consumptive, fevered, got up at five or six, walked through the icy cloisters to choir, and shivered with cold during the hours she spent there. She worked all day as if it was nothing, and in the evening she chanted the divine office until eleven.

Toil done, the poor little sister laboriously returned to her room stopping at each step to catch her breath. Her strength nearly spent, it sometimes took her an hour to get undressed. And after so many difficulties, she slept on a hard mattress resting on boards. Insomnia, coughing, feverish—she waited for daybreak and her daily harness.

When one compassionate sister suggested that she go to the infirmary where the surroundings were less primitive, she answered, "I am very happy to suffer alone; here, no one hears me coughing and I don't disturb anyone; as soon as I complain and am loaded with tendernesses, I am no longer joyful."

It was good that she could be joyful, because the care she received was practically nil. But she never dreamed of complaining.

"God sees all," she said. "I abandon myself to Him. He will inspire our Mother to look after me if it is necessary."[26]

As Mother Agnes of Jesus gently reproached her late for having kept her sickness hidden, the servant of God answered, "Oh, Mother, give thanks to God for it! Knowing my state and seeing me then so little cared for, you would have been too grieved by it!"

Finally, Therese's weak constitution succumbed despite her vigor. All the dispensations, all the alleviations, were then accorded her. But it was too late. Therese could no longer benefit from them.

Gentle as a lamb, she refrained from alluding to her neglect. On the contrary, her heart overflowed with gratitude.

"Dear Mother," she wrote her prioress, "the care you procured for me during my illness has taught me a great lesson in charity. No medication seemed too expensive; and if it did not help, without losing patience, you would try something else. When I would go to recreation, there was no attention you did not give me to keep me covered and out of the draft.

"Mother, I feel that I ought to be just as compassionate for the spiritual infirmities of my Sisters as you have been for my physical infirmity."

These words prove that if Mother Mary of Gonzaga had little discernment, her good intentions could not be doubted. By her blindness, she had been a docile instrument in the hands of providence desirous of developing the future saint.

In July, the invalid was finally taken to the infirmary.

When she saw her empty room, knowing her little sister would never return, Mother Agnes of Jesus said, "How grieved I shall be to look at that cell when you are no longer with us!"

"Be consoled, Mother, to think that I am going to be very happy up there; and to know that a great part of my happiness I have acquired in that little cell because," glancing toward heaven, "I have suffered much there; I would have been happy to die there!"[27]

No one ever surmised this, however, because the courageous nun hid her afflictions so well.

"When I suffer much," she confided to her eldest sister, "when painful and disagreeable things happen to me instead of looking sad I respond with a smile."

Mislead by her radiant appearance, the infirmary attendant said to her one day, "They claim that you have never suffered anything?"

Smiling, showing her a glass of sparkling red liquid, the obliging saint answered, "Look at this little glass; one would think it was full of a delicious wine. In reality, I have never taken anything more bitter.

"Well, it is the picture of my life; in the eyes of others, it was always clothed in brilliant colors; it seemed to them that I was drinking a choice liquid; and it was bitterness.

"I say 'bitterness' and still my life was not bitter because I have found my joy and my peace in all bitterness."[28]

In this quiet, smiling heroism, the little flower of Jesus blossomed in the shadow of the cross bedewed by his gracious tears and divine blood, basking in the radiance of his adorable face.

Practical Application

If anyone wishes to be my disciple, he must renounce himself, take up his cross and follow me,"[29] says the Lord.

Not content with making this renouncement a counsel, He made a still more rigorous precept.

"If you do not do penance," He warned, "you will all perish."[30]

Mortification, then, is not optional, practiced only by those who would emulate St. Therese of the Child Jesus in some cloister. No, penance is an essential and primordial duty for all Christians.

It is unfortunate that the type of training of many children today does not develop this strength of character which wants to make sacrifices for the love of God.

"In our day, they wanted an easy wat to sanctity," protested the Reverend Martial Lekeux.[31]

This was certainly not the case with Therese. In this chapter, we have seen the severity to which the courageous nun subjected her body.

These examples prove that the little way of Therese, as easy as it seemed, did not turn her away from the austere evangelical path.

We are reminded that if we wish to be like St. Therese of the Child Jesus, we must take courage and generously mortify ourselves:

(1) by the exercise of corporal penance (mortifications of all kinds) in keeping with the duties of our state in life and as our health permits;

(2) by a number of little mortifications of the senses, all of which are harmful to no one, but are very meritorious in the sight of God, and are eminently suitable for training the will;

(3) in accepting all the unpleasant things that Providence sends us in a spirit of co-redemption. On this subject, the great apostle opens to us an unexpected horizon.

"I fill up in my flesh," he said, "those things that are lacking to the sufferings of Christ for His body which is the Church."[32]

Since we do not wish to go into theolgical proofs, let it suffice simply to draw the following conclusion: in establishing His Church, whose members we are by the grace of God, Jesus Christ forms a mystical body "of which He is the Head."[33]

And just as in a human body no member can act unless the head is the driving force so it can be said that Christ sanctifies all circumstances and all sufferings.

So, by our affiliation with the soul of the Church and our incorporation into His mystical body, we indirectly collaborate with Christ in the work of redemption.

The more resigned that collaboration and the more it costs, the more we become united with Jesus in an expiatory and efficacious manner.

Considered from this spiritual point of view, suffering—whatever it might be—takes on a resplendant light. And our bodies—instead of grieving us—will gladden because we have the freedom of collaborating with Jesus as instruments of love, "like a humanity on the increase in which He renews all His mystery."[34]

COLLOQUY: With Jesus Crucified.

Crushed in the winepress of pain
  I have proved
All of my love for Thee.
To sacrifice self each day is my joy,
No other delight for me.

St. Therese of the Child Jesus

Notes

1. Dom Gueranger, *The Liturgical Year*.
2. "Hail, Holy Cross."
3. Madame Martin died piously at the age of 46, August 28, 1887. Therese was then four years old.
4. Deposition at the Apostolic Process, p. 125.
5. From a manuscript at the Abbey of Notre Dame du Pre.
6. Canon Delatroette, pastor of St. James Parish in Lisieux.
7. II Cor. 7:5.
8. Her sister Leonie.
9. Marie Guerin, who eventually joined them in Carmel.
10. *Summarium of 1919*, p. 509.
11. *Story of a Soul*, Ch. 12.
12. Monsignor Laveille, *Vie de Sainte Therese de l'Enfant Jesus,* p. 307. It seems that Therese may eventually have relaxed a little on this point because the diary of Mother Agnes of Jesus cites numerous words of Therese which clearly take on a confidential tone.
13. It would seem more prudent to us, considering the weakness of human nature, to reveal quite simply grave illnesses to those whom it may concern.
14. *L'Esprit de Ste. Therese de l'Enfant Jesus*, p. 47.
15. *Summarium of 1919*, p. 203.
16. *L'Esprit de Ste. Therese de l'Enfant Jesus*, p. 172.
17. *Story of a Soul*, Ch. 12.
18. *L'Esprit de Ste. Therese de l'Enfant Jesus*, pp. 172–173.
19. *Story of a Soul*, Ch. 12.
20. We must not lose sight of the fact that in matters of mortification, above all, the saints sometimes gave us examples which were more to be admired than imitated.

21. *Summarium of 1919*, p. 623.
22. One must consider this from a supernatural point of view in order to realize the hundredfold promised to religious in the Gospel.
23. *Vie de Ste. Therese de l'Enfant Jesus*, pp. 310–311.
24. Conseils et Souvenirs, p. 277.
25. *Story of A Soul*, Ch. 12.
26. *Summarium of 1919*, p. 493.
27. *Story of a Soul*, Ch. 12.
28. Ibid.
29. Matt. 16:24.
30. Luke 13:3.
31. In a book entitled *Maggy*.
32. Col. 1:24.
33. Col. 1:18.
34. Sr. Elizabeth of the Trinity.

Chapter Twelve
Her Monastic Virtues

Lord, if You cherich the purity of the angel
whose bright spirit is clothed in innocence,
do You not also hold dear the lilly springing
out of the mire and which Your love has seen
fit to keep pure?

St. Therese of the Child Jesus

"Truly, Sr. Therese of the Child Jesus is remarkable! She shows us up in everything," said those religious who witnessed her fervent beginnings.[1]

The mistress of novices marveled at the religious spirit of this fifteen-year-old child, declaring, "There is a sort of majesty in her bearing which inspires respect, and she truly grows in wisdom and grace before God and the community."[2]

Such a nun so completely faultless had to excel in what was essentially evangelical perfection, the practice of the three virtues—poverty, chastity, obedience.

Her poverty

Therese had refined, delicate tastes. Silk, satin, gold, lace—none of these would have looked out of place on her. The most artistic objects could have ideally surrounded her.

But desiring only to please Christ by the practice of poverty, the servant of God forever renounced the tinsel and baubles of

France when she divested herself of her elaborate bridal dress on the day she took the habit.[3]

The community clothed her in a robe of rough serge, badly tailored. Asked if this was not contrary to her good taste, she answered joyfully, "It makes no more difference than if it were the dress of a Chinaman two thousand miles away!"

Her sandals were so worn that they were twisted, cramping her walking.

At length, she artfully mentioned to the seamstress, "You will give me the most patched and oldest linen, won't you? That's what I prefer."

In things given her, she was reminded of her love for poverty. When a pretty pitcher was removed from her cell and replaced by an old chipped water jug, she was delighted.

Even the lamp wick she used could only be pulled up with a pin. It was tedious and unnerving. Though she never tried to have it replaced. One evening, she did not find the wick on its accustomed shelf. Rather than break silence to reclaim it, she spent an hour in the darkness of her cell, savoring the poverty which deprived her of even necessary things.

The servant of God showed that she was a worthy emulator of St. John of the Cross who rose in the middle of the night in order not to keep an extra pin on his monastic habit.

One evening, Therese laid a pen knife at the door of her cell. When asked why, she replied, "It is not something that belongs in the cell, and as I have not had the time to put it back in its place, I fear that it would not be poverty to keep it."

This was, perhaps, a little excessive. But it nevertheless indicates the love that Therese had for the virtue of poverty.

When Celine entered the Carmel of Lisieux,—the gracious saint, in her usual kindliness, gave up her holy water font and her inkstand, replacing them with objects she found in the attic.

Not content to do without all comfort, the servant of God understood that diligent work consisted in earning her bread by the sweat of her brow, an obligation for one who professes voluntary poverty for Christ.

Although it cost her much at times, since she was more used to being waited upon than waiting on others, she went about her daily tasks with pleasure, quite a master of herself for a girl of fifteen years.

During her postulancy, Mother Mary of Gonzaga, hardly finding any justifiable corrections to give her, berated her for "her slowness, and the lack of zeal with which she went about her duties."

Therese took these reproaches seriously. Trying to redeem herself, she tied herself down for a long time to manual work during the cherished hour of free time.

"Thinking that such was the desire of our Mother," she said, "I plied my little needle without raising my eyes; but as I wished to be faithful and act only under the glance of Jesus, nobody every knew about it."

Eventually, the alacrity of her religious life was uninterrupted. "We are poor," she said. "Time does not belong to us."

The whole day, excepting choir time, she tirelessly manipulated brooms, brushes, pens, needles.

Is that how one hurries when she has children (souls) to feed!" she said quickly, once chiding a novice who was sauntering on her way to the laundry.

Her pencils were used to the very end. Her autobiography— that work which revolutionized sanctity in the world—was written on two pitiful notebooks that a servant would have scorned.

In a spirit of poverty,[4] she never asked for permission to write her poems as they came to her. She waited until the hour of free time given the nuns after compline. Then she took great pains to recall exactly what she had composed in the morning.

Her poems were scrawled hurriedly on old envelopes. She then gave them to the first person she saw, depriving herself of keeping a copy of her work.

Therese kept her heart free of all sense of ownership. She gave whatever she had with such good grace, no matter how inconvenient for her, that her sisters did not hesitate to come back again and again.

She deprived herself of even the most necessary objects, considering herself "happy to be relieved of them." Then she sang.

> To the Heart Divine e'er burning
>   with tenderness
> I have given my all . . . swiftly
>   I run . . .
> A single wealth is all I possess
> To live of Love!

Although the vow of poverty is to renounce material possessions, Therese practiced the virtue of poverty to such an extent that she was even detached from her own thoughts and inspirations.

During recreation, she would quietly communicate a light she had received in prayer or come out with a witty rejoinder for which she was noted. When her neighbor claimed it as if it had been her own, she tolerated it. This was done to amuse onlookers at Therese's expense. What did this nonsensical self-love mean to a soul so detached as the servant of God?

"I find it all very natural that that Sister should claim something belonging to me as her own," she explained. "This thought belongs to the Holy Spirit and it is not mine since St. Paul affirms that we cannot, without this spirit of love, call God 'Father.'"[5]

She did not even claim goods of spiritual nature as her own. And although her works were strictly personal, she gave a large part of them as satisfaction and expiation for her neighbor.

"If I had been rich," she acknowledged, "I would not have been able to see a poor person without giving him an alms. I do the same in my spiritual life; I give all in proportion to souls so that I have not yet found time to say: "Now, I am going to work for myself!'"

When Sr. Marie of the Sacred Heart, told Therese about the sisterly envy she felt at the special graces with which the Lord filled her, she responded, "To tell the truth, that is what can be called 'the wages given to an unjust steward'[6] if the person concerned is proudly complaisant in it. Oh! I feel that is not what pleases God at all in my soul. What pleases Him is to see me love my littleness, my poverty; it is the blind hope I have in His mercy. That is my only treasure, dear Godmother; why can't it be yours?"

During her last illness, the mortified Carmelite begged her sisters not to go to much expense buying her medicine. She was resigned, however, when she learned that St. Gertrude rejoiced in a similar situation, because she valued the merit which would come to the benefactors of her monastery.

Once her family brought her some chilled liquor and savory grapes. Therese was feverish and thirsty, yet she never claimed these refreshments for herself.

When Sr. Marie of the Sacred Heart seemed surprised at this, she said to her quite simply, "A little beggar has the right to beg for what is necessary, but not for what is superfluous."[7]

It was necessary to specify whether it was truly a luxury for her to quench her thirst in this manner. But the vocabulary of generosity among saints is unintelligible, not often understood by mediocre Christians.

Although her entire body was bruised by the scaldings of her treatments, Therese began sleeping on the bare floor without matress or pad.

"After she was spoken to quite sternly on this point," reported Sr. Genevieve of the Holy Face, "Therese slept on her straw mat during the night. Since I did not have permission to give her a mattress (I was then an aide in the infirmary) I had no other recourse than to fold a big cover in fourths and to put it under her sheet."[8]

When Mother Agnes of Jesus showed sadness at seeing her sister accept so many privations, Therese said, "Don't worry about me, please! I am still very much cared for!"

Despite her constant discomfort and consuming fever, the courageous patient still desired to serve her community as much as her strength would allow. So she was invariably busy.

"I always have to have some work in my hand," she confided, "In that way, I am not disturbed and I never lose time."

Her chastity

"Where does that child get her angelic expression?" asked a friend of the Martin family. "There are other little girls with features just as refined but this one has heaven in her eyes."

The good lady was right. Therese was angelic. This soul, so marvelously pure, felt exiled in her body.

"I have always been ill at ease in my body," she confided. "Even at a tender age I was conscious of it."[9]

From the age of two, her heart was drawn spontaneously to the spouse of virgins. The virginity of the adolescent Therese is seen in this hymn.

> He has already set a sign upon my face
>   So that I may admit no other love
> My heart is buoyed up by the tender grace
>   Of my loving King above.
>
> When I love Jesus Christ and when we meet
>   My heart becomes more pure, and more chaste still
> And in virginity, His kiss so sweet
>   Is a treasure none can fill.

She never allowed her heart to become unduly attached. At boarding school, she guarded herself against foolish attachments to her teachers. In Carmel she kept watch over her heart so not to become too fond of her prioress, Mother Mary of Gonzaga. Still, the chastity of the virgin of Lisieux had to be tested.

The diocesan pilgrimage which brought Therese to Rome was made up of well-to-do families. And one can suppose that the topics of conversation were not always edifying.

Numerous nude statues were displayed in museums and public places as well as in certain Italian sanctuaries. These often presented spectacle for the innocent eyes of a child.

Therese had a vague foreboding of these dangers. So before leaving for Rome, she recommended herself as a timid dove to our Lady of victories.

"Since I never knew evil," she confided, "I was afraid of finding it; I had not experienced 'that to the pure all things are pure.' "[10]

During the journey, two misadventures happened to her. When the travelers stepped from the train at Bologna, they became surrounded by a crowd of students whose enthusiasm was impetuously Italian.

One stared at Therese boldly, took hold of her, and swept her off to the other side of the tracks. But she recommended herself to the Blessed Virgin, giving him such a withering look that he withdrew confused.[11]

A more subtle temptation befell her a little later. A young pilgrim of faultless distinction noticed the ravishing beauty of little Therese and became markedly attentive to her. Mastering her heart, Therese kept her reserve, but it was painful as she confidentially acknowledged to Celine.

"Oh! it is high time that Jesus withdraws me from the poisoned breath of the world! I feel that my heart is easily drawn to affection; and where others perish I too would perish because I am the weakest of creatures."[12]

She attributed her innocence to a very special prevenient grace of Christ, adding, "With my ardent nature and my affectionate heart, I would be capable of falling lower than Magdalene."

God rewarded these humble dispositions and spared her from every interior suggestion contrary to chastity. An aura of purity seemed to surround her, and all who came near her were imbued with holy respect for her.

Her monastic reserve made her timid toward persons on the outside.

Returning from the parlor once, having practically said nothing as was her custom, she made this reflection.

"How quiet I was this afternoon in the parlor! And yet, almost immediately afterwards I had to reprimand a novice very severely; I do not recognize myself! How my character changes! My timidity arises from an extreme uneasiness which I experience when someone pays attention to me."

Despite her self-effacement, she was constantly asked for advice. She was so chaste and simple that one could confide to her any temptation, knowing she would not be disturbed by it.

Therese was not invulnerable to these things by nature. But she had placed her innocence under the protection of the Blessed Virgin and St. Joseph. Sure of their protection, she remained in peace even in the presence of dangerous occasions.[13]

Her clear-sightedness enabled her to quickly recognize the traps which the demon set to snare her virtue. Her struggle here gives her merit.

She wrote to a soul being tempted, "The purest hearts are sometimes the most tried, they are often in darkness. They then believe that they have lost their innocence and think that the thorns which surround them have torn their crown to pieces. But no, the lilies in the midst of the thorns are best preserved; it is in them that Jesus takes His delight: 'happy the man who stands firm when trials come.'"[14]

She even said to Celine, "Make of your heart a flower-bed where our sweet Lord comes to take His repose, planting there beautiful lilies of innocence because we are virgins ... and then, let us not forget that 'virginity is a deep silence of all earthly cares,' not only useless cares, but all cares."

And in a letter dated 1891, we read, "What a grace to be a virgin, to be the Spouse of Jesus! It must be very sublime since the purest, the most intelligent of all creatures would have preferred to remain a virgin rather than become the Mother of God if in doing so she would have had to sacrifice her virginity."

This angelic nun wished to participate in the fruitful virginity of Mary in some way. This desire is found again in one of her poems.

I am a virgin, O Jesus! united to Thee,
Yet a mother of souls; O divine mystery!

Ever referring to the "white lilies of the valley." she became so impregnated by their purity that she gave her affections free rein in a spiritual manner.

"I no longer feel that it is necessary for me to refuse consolations of the heart," she declared, "'for my heart is established in God.'[15] Because He has singularly loved it, it has grown by degrees giving to those dear to me an incomparable tenderness even deeper than if it was concentrated in a selfish and fruitless affection."

In Christ, with him and through him, this virgin tenderly loved her sisters, still keeping her lilylike purity.

With graceful symbolism this is called to mind.

Jesus, I am Your living temple pure
   That nothing evil can profane, defile;
Dwell in my heart; is it not a garden sure
   Of which each flower turns to You the while?
But if You stay e'er far from me,
   O white lily of the valley,
I know full well my petals dropped will be
   Always, my well-Beloved, Thee,
      Jesus, scented lily,
      Flower in me!

Her obedience

"How happy are the simple religious," wrote St. Therese of the Child Jesus, "since their only guide is the will of their superiors they are sure of not being deceived. But when they cease to consult this infallible guide, then the soul promptly strays into dry paths where the waters of grace are soon found lacking to her."

This was not her case. Entering the cloister, she renounced her liberty into the maternal hands of her superiors. God permitted that. They exercised the young postulant vigorously, at the same time feeling sympathy for her.

To make Therese's obedience shine in all its splendor, it is necessary to study the characters of the two religious in charge.

"The Mistress of Novices,"[16] wrote Therese, "was a real saint; the archtype of the first Carmelites. Her kindness towards me left nothing to be desired; I loved her very much. I appreciated her and yet my heart did not expand under her guidance."

A lack of discernment on the part of the directress caused this. Not understanding the attraction which swayed the soul of Therese, she tried to indoctrinate her with tedious sermons. The opening of the beginner's heart was further complicated because of the incompatibility of spirit between the mistress and Therese. These two souls, though both beautiful, esteemed, without understanding, each other. Despite her good will, Therese considered the times appointed her for direction and spiritual counseling "a kind of tedious martyrdom," when it should have given her comfort.

With the prioress, St. Therese of the Child Jesus fared no better. There is no doubt that prioress Mother Mary of Gonzaga, of the noble Calvados family, held sympathy and spiritual affinity for Therese. Along with her rare qualities of initiative and know-how, she possessed a personal charm that was the product of a first-class education. But this active, richly endowed nature had many gaps in it. Impressionable, suspicious, predisposed to melancholy—she did not always possess balance and consistency which make government a blessing.

Therese learned this at her own expense. The mother prioress—desiring to put such an exceptionally precocious vocation to the test—as we have already said,[17] mortified the young postulant on every occasion.

The Reverend Godefroy Madeleine,[18] extraordinary confessor to the community, had this to say.

"Mother Mary of Gonzaga confided to me that in order to exercise the virtue of Sr. Therese she schooled herself in putting her to the test and so pretended to be indifferent and severe with her. She attested to me besides that the apparent severity had certainly been very trying to the servant of God, but that the pain which Therese experienced because of it had never deterred her from practicing perfect obedience."[19]

When the admonitions of the prioress became too strong, the poor little novice sought refuge near her mistress. And without criticism, she acknowledged her anxiety.

"I can still see her," affirmed Sr. Marie of the Angels, "coming to confide her troubled heart to me one day without letting the least complaint escape her. She discerned the workings of God in her soul and smiled in spite of it all."[20]

On account of this strained situation, obedience was not exactly a cure-all for the amiable saint. Nevertheless, she never exempted herself from it.

"Our Mistress," recounted Therese, "had told me during my postulancy to let her know every time I was sick to my stomach. This happened every day. When this nausea took hold of me, I would have preferred to be struck a hundred times with a stick than to be obligated to tell her; but, nevertheless, I told her each time under obedience. Sr. Marie of the Angels, who did not remember giving me the order, would say to me: 'My poor child, you will never have the necessary health to follow the Rule; it is too much for you.' And she would run off to get me some remedies.

"Mother Mary of Gonzaga, who was astonished and displeased with the daily recital of my complaints, would quickly reply: 'This child is always complaining! One comes to Carmel to suffer; if she cannot take more than that, then she must be ill!' I still continued to admit to having stomachaches for a long time out of pure obedience, even at the risk of being sent home until in God's good time I no longer had to make this acknowledgement."[21]

At times, the prioress exercised authority even more arbitrarily. During a retreat preached by the Reverend Alexis, a Franciscan from Caen, she forbid St. Therese of the Child Jesus to consult the retreat master, though the other sisters were permitted to. She therefore deprived the servant of God of spiritual help necessary for her, because Therese was in great spiritual distress at the time. The young religious suffered from this but submitted without complaining.

Despite the obvious incompetence of her prioress, the servant of God saw her as "the representative of God." This was enough for Therese to respect and love her. Therese had a clear idea of the silent reproaches heaped upon the prioress because of her irregular government. And she took it in stride to be the one to console her, to surround her with filial tenderness, even to enlighten her.

It is no wonder that Mother Mary of Gonzaga delightfully acknowledged to some of the sisters, "Therese is a treasure to have in Carmel, the best of the lot, an angel!"

What can be said of the fidelity of the holy Carmelite to the least general recommendations made to the Community? The prioress had the habit of making many little rules which she soon forgot and which fell into disuse. But St. Therese of the Child Jesus strove to observe them until they had been explicitly dispensed with. One old sister noticed her admirable fidelity on this point, considering her a saint. She was for all her sisters a model of obedience.

"Never," declared one of them, "have I seen her commit the smallest infraction of the Rule. At the first sound of the bell, she stopped whatever she was doing, even when in the middle of an interesting conversation. If she were sewing, she dropped her needle without even finishing the stitch she had begun."[22]

Sr. Marie of the Angels, in her deposition at the canonical process, recounted an incident which backs up this.

"One winter day, as it was permitted, Therese took off her heavy rough stockings which were very damp in order to dry them near the fire during recreation when someone came to tell her that the sacristy bell was ringing as this was her charge. She simply put on her sandals and walked through the two cloisters unaware of her imprudent exposure to the icy wind.

"How many others would have asked for a moment's delay! For her, God had spoken; she ran to the call of duty without the least hesitation."

At times, obedience made her pay dearly.

Therese had an aversion to spiders, but during a great part of her monastic life she had to pursue them relentlessly. One need only recall the public reprimand Mother Mary of Gonzaga gave her, ordering her to dislodge the cobwebs in the cloister.

The day after her clothing, St. Therese of the Child Jesus was given the charge of sweeping the refectory everyday along with a little nook adjacent to it, called St. Alexis, This room, situated partly under a particularly dusty and dark staircase, held a den of spiders. So the novice had sufficient reason for refusing to exterminate these repugnant creatures.

During the forty hours devotion in 1891, the convent charges were changed, and the servant of God held the duties of sacristan and portress, she was then entrusted with guarding the safe where important papers and the community's expense account were kept. After this, she was appointed to paint a fresco of angels which adorns the inner oratory of the Lisieux Carmel.

Shortly after her election as prioress, Mother Agnes of Jesus imposed on her young sister an unexpected act of obedience.

One evening, Therese reminiscing with her sisters about some of the happiest moments of her childhood, Sr. Marie of the Sacred Heart took the prioress aside and said to her, "Our little sister is an angel who is not long for this world, and you will be sorry later to have lost for us such interesting remembrances."

Mother Agnes of Jesus thought about this a few weeks, then ordered Therese to write her autobiography.

Therese began the task immediately. On the eve of the feast of St. Agnes, it was completed. Going to evening prayer, she passed and knelt before the prioress, as was the custom. Humbly, Therese placed these precious pages on her stall.

Reading the manuscript, Mother Agnes of Jesus foresaw the immense good that a book of this kind would produce in souls. Knowing the deep humility of the servant of God, she did not hesitate to make her a part of this idea of publishing the manuscript and of asking her advice on it.

"Mother," she answered, "after my death, it will not be necessary to speak to anyone about my manuscript until it is published. If you do otherwise, or if you delay its publication, the devil will set many a snare for you in order to thwart the work of God . . . such an important work!"

The advice was followed. After the imprimatur of Bishop Hugonin was obtained on March 8, 1898, *The Story of a Soul* appeared the following October. A few weeks later, publication would have been impossible.[23]

The fervent nun not only obeyed her superiors but her companions as well, even when her orders seemed unreasonable.

Since she was second portress, she was asked one evening to prepare an outside night lamp, though she did not have the necessary tools to work with.

To satisfy this unnecessary request, the servant of God realized that she would have to sacrifice her hour of free time. This infringement on her time cost so much that she begged for grace. But Therese, reluctant, conscientiously set herself to the prescribed task.

"In order to conquer myself," she confided, "I pretended that I was preparing a night lamp for the Blessed Virgin and the Child Jesus; then I did it with incredible care leaving not the least speck of dust, and little by little I felt a deep peace and a great sweetness in my soul.

"The bell rang for Matins and I would not have been able to follow suit had I not received such a grace so that if Sr. X had come and told me that I was mistaken and that it was necessary to prepare another night lamp, I would have happily obeyed.

"From that day, I have resolved never to take into consideration if the things commanded were useful or not."

One novice resisted the yoke of obedience and subordination

and reasonably alleged that she obey only her immediate superiors.

The young mistress said to her with that serene conviction which comes only with experience, "When one is humble, she acknowledges willingly that everyone can have authority over her."

In fact, we have seen that Therese practiced what she preached. The following incident bears this out.

One evening during her last illness, the community gathered in a hermitage at a corner of the garden to sing a hymn.

Although already racked by fever, St. Therese of the Child Jesus dragged herself along. When she got there, she was so spent that she sat down. One of her overly zealous companions signaled for her to get up. "We saw how she obeyed immediately," recalled her contemporaries, "and in spite of her weariness and exhaustion she remained standing till the end of the hymn."

During her last days, temperature rising and fever overpowering her, her sister Marie wanted to make her cooler by lifting the sheet and coverlet laying over her feet.

Therese stopped her, saying, "I would like it, but I don't think it is permitted. Ask our Mother."

Indeed, Mother Mary of Gonzaga at times told her religious that it was more perfect to keep their woolen covers on even in the summer. Therese, even on her deathbed, took these remarks seriously, even though they no longer applied to her.

Asked toward the end if she did not regret that Mother Agnes of Jesus was no longer prioress, she answered with an angelic smile, "Oh! no; on the contrary, I am very happy to have such a great opportunity of exercising the spirit of faith by dying in the arms of another Prioress."

Practical Application

Lesson in poverty. Not all men will be poor by reason of vow or through necessity. Neither will they be protected by that awesome evangelical utterance, "It is difficult for a rich man to enter the Kingdom of Heaven."[24]

If it is necessary for us to use the goods of this world, let us do so with moderation, like a bank deposit confided to our care, for which we must give an account.

We must take this revenue and deduct from it a large part to support the needy and apostolic works, particularly the missions.

Let us follow the advice given by St. Therese of the Child Jesus, a soul who did all she could to acquire graces, merits, and virtues.

"You said that you wanted to imitate me; do you not know though that I am very poor? It is God Who gives me just what is necessary to sanctify me." She declared, "God rejoices even more in a soul humbly resigned to her poverty than in the creation of myriads of stars and the scope of the heavens."

Then let us give stars to God in this manner. We will lose nothing by it because He says through his Son, "Blessed are the poor in spirit for theirs is the Kingdom of Heaven."[25]

Lesson in chastity. Little St. Therese of Lisieux showed us four ways to preserve and increase this angelic virtue—prayer, vigilance, mortification, humility.

Let us put them faithfully into practice, and our soul will be surrounded by that spiritual clear-sightedness and that interior light which made the virgin apostle exclaim, "It is the Lord!"[26] Although the other apostles did not discern Him.

"Blessed are the pure of heart for they shall see God."[27]

Lesson in obedience. At times, we have perhaps told ourselves, "Yes, I would obey willingly, provided that the one who commands me is capable of governing and commands only those things which are useful and reasonable."

But would this not be entirely natural? What merit is there in doing the will of another because it pleases you? Is it then only man whom you will obey and not the representative of God?

Let us consider the supernatural obedience of Therese. At times she was given foolish or contradictory orders. Her superior was whimsical, authoritative. But the servant of God did not falter.

Not a murmur, not a criticism, no rebellion. It sufficed that this person was her legitimate superior. For this, she respected and obeyed her.

If she was treated well, it was the hand of God who caressed her. If she was treated badly, it was the hand of God who chastised her. But she always welcomed it with love.

We admire this splendid example. Let us imitate it and we will be eminently pleasing to God and profit from it, since heaven is reserved for "the obedient man to sing his victories."

COLLOQUY: With St. Therese of the Child Jesus.

> The angel proud, in the bosom of light
>   Cried out 'I will not obey!'
> But I on earth cried out in the night:
>   'I surrender my will each day.'
> I feel in myself a boldness divine,
> To battle the fury of hell;
> Obedience—the armor I claim as mine
> Is the shield of my heart as well.
>
> *St. Therese of the Child Jesus*

Notes

1. *Summarium of 1914*, p. 679.
2. Deposition at the Apostolic Process, p. 215.
3. Monsieur Martin had wanted "his little queen" to be dressed in white velvet decorated with swans and lace. Her long hair fell over her shoulders, and lilies completed her virginal attire.
4. The rule of Carmel considers it an exercise of poverty that one does not have free time at her disposal.
5. Romans 8:15.

6. Luke 16:2.
7. *Summarium of 1919*, p. 402.
8. Ibid., p. 394.
9. Monsignor Laveille, *Biographie de Sainte Therese de l'Enfant Jesus,* p. 303.
10. Tit. 1:15.
11. *Summarium of 1919*, p. 398.
12. Ibid., p. 632.
13. *Biographie de Sainte Therese de l'Enfant Jesus,* p. 303.
14. *Summarium of 1919*, p. 400.
15. Office of St. Agnes.
16. Sr. Marie of the Angels.
17. See Ch. 6, p. 65.
18. Abbot of St. Michel de Frigolet. Afterwards Abbot of the Premontres de Mondaye (Calvados).
19. Deposition of the Apostolic Process, p. 731.
20. Ibid., p. 665.
21. *Summarium of 1919*, p. 518.
22. Ibid., p. 418.
23. *Vie de Sainte Therese de l'Enfant Jesus*, p. 362.
24. Matt. 19:23.
25. Ibid., 5:3.
26. John 21:7.
27. Matt. 5:8.

Chapter Thirteen
Her Prudence in the Direction of Souls

> Ah! Souls would arrive at great sanc-
> tity if, from the beginning, they were
> well directed!
>
> *St. Therese of the Child Jesus*

In February 1893, Mother Mary of Gonzaga's six-year term as prioress was up, and the community elected Mother Agnes of Jesus in her place.

Not wanting to take all authority away from the former prioress, Mother Agnes appointed her mistress of novices. But to off-set her rather chimerical temperament, she appointed St. Therese of the Child Jesus her assistant, whose proven virtue, tact, and discernment she knew well.

In effect, Therese was a go-between, placed, in a sense, be-tween the devil and the deep blue sea. Though her privileges were not clearly defined, she assumed more duties than rights and was frequently hindered by having to humor the ex-prioress.

This situation was even more complicated three years later, when Mother Mary of Gonzaga was again made head of the monastery and continued to head the novitiate at the same time. Until her death Therese remained a subordinate, and trained the novices only under the whimsical control of the prioress. To accept this state of affairs without meeting conflict, one had to be a saint. But the servant of God took a point of view, simplifying everything.

"Let us make ourselves so little that we can be trampled under foot without even giving the appearance that we are aware of it," she recommended.

Moreover, she allowed Mother Mary of Gonzaga to think herself the principle cause of all the good which took place in the novitiate.

"Mother, you are the one who represents to me the precious brush held lovingly in the hand of Jesus when He wishes to do great things in the souls of your children," she wrote, "but as for me, I am the very little one that He deigns to use afterwards for the smaller details."

Therese certainly had no desire to be put on a pedestal or to possess authority, because she saw in this serious trouble.

Having compared herself to "a bowl which little kittens eat out of," risking being broken, she added, "To tell the truth, the danger is not that great with me because I'm placed at the bottom—on the floor. It's not the same thing with Prioresses, though: since their places are at table, they meet up with many more perils. Ah! what poisonous praises are served daily to those who hold the first places! What deadly fragrance! And how necessary it is for a soul to be detached from itself."

"Most privileges are those which God keeps for Himself alone. How many outstanding souls require a miracle of grace in order to preserve their lustre!"

Our Lord did not hesitate to perform this miracle favoring his little spouse. To the amiable candor of childhood, she enjoined the "prudence of old men"[1] and showed herself capable.

Her novices, some imperfect as they were in the beginning, became so fervent under her direction that they soon formed a select group from which a springtime of vitality and perfection developed for the Carmel of Lisieux.

Her supernatural direction

From the beginning, the young mistress of novices understood "that to do good to souls without divine help is as impossible as to expect the sun to shine in the night."

Why? Because a supernatural act is not worked out in purely human ways. It is necessary God surround it beforehand with his all-powerful strength.

"If the Lord Himself does not build the house, in vain do the workers toil."[2]

In virtue of this principle, the servant of God—notwithstanding her maternal role—resolved to remain always little. Nestling as a child in the arms of the builder and divine shepherd, she begged that she might build the spiritual edifice of her daughter and be able to nourish "her little lambs."

This contract was sealed in the intimacy of her communion with the beloved.

From then on, the daily tasks seemed simplified to Therese. She was content to remain united with our Lord. And gradually, one hungry little lamb after another coming to her, the good shepherd filled the hand of Therese.

At times the little lamb bounded with joy when the food served appeared succulent. Other times it wore a sad face, as if fasting. But the obliging shepherdess, careful not to give in to her little lamb, fashioned a menu suited to her need.

"Bitter herbs are a medicinal property that one appreciates only after having tasted it," she said.

For peace's sake, the little reluctant lamb had to be content.

Our Lord was truly the essence of Therese's direction. Her replies bore the authentic stamp of divine wisdom.

The prudent mistress was not ignorant that, conforming to the law, the privileges of the superiors of religious women came to one thing: observance of the rule and inculcating into their novices the spirit of their order.

Respecting their freedom of conscience, she willingly placed herself at the disposal of those who, desiring to profit fully from her insight, allowed her to penetrate deeper into their souls.

At times Jesus revealed to her by intuition, the interior faults which one of her daughters hid. It was then easy for her to enlighten and console the soul which God had just unmasked.

In order to keep her direction on a supernatural plane, St. Therese of the Child Jesus, while conversing with her novices, constantly disciplined her natural curiosity because, she claimed, "No one can do good to souls when she seeks herself."

Prayer was her chief weapon in times of spiritual combat. Thanks to this, she obtained unexpected conversions as in the case of the young novice who, after receiving a somewhat harsh reprimand, departed in a huff, telling Therese, "I am going to find our Mother (the pseudo novice mistress, Mother Mary of Gonzaga) and I will let her know that I will never again seek the advice of Sr. Therese of the Child Jesus."

Next day she returned full of contrition to find her holy mistress and said to her, "You had every reason to be severe yesterday; at first, I rebelled, then I felt that you were praying for me; at that time, I recalled it all, and I saw that you were very just. Now I come to you so that you will enlighten me entirely."

Not content with appeasing rebellious souls, Therese's prayer revitalized sinking courage. Here is an example.

After an exhausting wash day, a young sister, overburdened with interior difficulties and fatigue, came looking for comfort from her angelic mistress. But the monastery clock had just struck, and the servant of God—always exact—said to her, "The bell is ringing for prayer; I do not have time to console you; besides, I see clearly that I would be dealing here with an unnecessary difficulty; God wants you to suffer only for a minute."

The novice went to choir so discouraged that for the first time since her entrance, she told herself, "I will never have the strength to be a Carmelite; it is too hard a life for me!"

Pondering this, suddenly an extraordinary change took place in her soul. Her vocation appeared as something beautiful to her. And she understood the price of suffering. The privations and fatigue of religious life seemed to her infinitely more dear than worldly satisfactions. She came away from prayer absolutely transformed.

Next day, the young sister recounting this incident, she saw that St. Therese of the Child Jesus was deeply moved and asked her why.

"How good God is!" Therese answered. "Yesterday evening, I felt so sorry for you that from the moment when we began our prayer I did not stop praying for you and asked Our Lord to console you, to change your mind and to show you the price of suffering. He has heard my prayer!"[3]

The saint asked God not to allow her daughters to become unduly attached to her. She obtained this favor and more. Yet even the most difficult novices began to feel veneration for their young mistress.

Indeed, the human heart, when its affections are regulated, does not waste away but is expanded. Its affections, enshrined in the gothic arch of divine love, are embellished with a hue resembling the stained glass windows of our churches—lusterless at night, resplendent at the rising sun.

Her discernment in the direction of souls

From childhood, Therese was noted for unusual perception. This natural wisdom served her well when she was placed in the delicate position of directing souls.

She began by declaring that in long lines of people, every person of the same category resembled each other. But taken individually, each one had different mind and character. She concluded from this that it would be foolish and utopian "to wish to lead all souls in the same manner."

With some, she made herself little, not hesitating to confide her personal difficulties. These souls, glad to learn that she had traveled the same path, took heart and followed her directives blindly.

With logical and practical souls, she appealed to their judgement and good sense.

With the more sensitive, she thought they would be more influenced by affective motives.

Certainly with hot-headed persons she was strict. Never did she go back on any decision. To humble herself would show weakness.

This severe system was especially imposed on her first two novices, both lay sisters, whose difficult dispositions needed much guidance.

Later on, she had more sensitive, generous souls to lead, making her task much easier.

There were as many purifying trials as there were diverse characters among her daughters. Some tended toward scruples, anxiety, a fear of damnation. Others, Sr. Genevieve of the Holy Face[4] for one, passed through long periods of painful aridity.

At times there were dark clouds to dissipate, temptations to moderate, jealousies and natural antipathies to combat.

"There was not one criticism against her person or her direction which the humble Mistress was not subjected to from time to time, the expression of which was as mortifying as it was unjustified."[5]

The valiant Carmelite did not become disconcerted by anything. She enlightened and encouraged tempted souls, and welcomed flattering confidences which beginners awkwardly made to her.

Her observations, always appropriate and made in a calm voice, were flavored at times with light humor.

A young sister boasted one day of having the same opinion about something as Therese.

"Ah!" cried St. Therese of the Child Jesus, "you are really putting yourself forward now! As for me, I am very careful of plying that trade; I prefer to repeat with Our Lord: 'I do not seek my own glory. Another will take care of it.'"[6]

Obviously, the servant of God did not hesitate to set herself up as a model, but it was with such simplicity that there was no trace of self-love in it. Besides, she was such a formidable adversary of vanity in others that she would not wish to tolerate this fault in herself.

Once, when a novice came looking for compliments, she refused, saying, "What is that little act of virtue compared to what Jesus has the right to expect of your fidelity. You ought rather to humble yourself for allowing so many occasions of proving your love for Him escape you."

She reproved another who worried excessively.

"You are wrong in thinking of what unfortunate thing can happen to you in the future; it is like getting yourself all tangled up in order to get straightened out."

Her most original intervention came when one of her daughters habitually cried over nothing.

Noticing among her painting materials a beautifully shaped shell, she said while holding it out to her, "From now on, you will collect all your tears in this shell."

From that time, when the great waters of tribulation threatened, the novice manipulated the little dish so quickly from one eye to the other that she soon forgot the cause of her grief.

Thanks to this ingenious strategy, the novice completely overcame her hypersensitivity.

Let us note in passing that such a predisposition to tears is very often caused by nervousness and can be combated more efficaciously by good nourishment, fresh air, and rest!

One of the principal means Therese used to influence her novices was by example.

In the course of a very tiring day, one put her young mistress to the test by purposely complicating her work.

"But not for one moment," she said, "was I able to find any fault in her. She was always very gracious and amiable, and did not show the slightest fatigue. What happened, I wondered: was she not well? She appeared to be spirited enough. Finally, I could stand it no longer and threw myself into her arms confiding to her all that was troubling my soul.

"How do you do it? I asked her; How do you practice such virtue that you can be constantly joyous, calm, and so much yourself?"

"I have not always been like this," she answered, "but since I never seek myself, I lead the happiest kind of life as you can see."

Could she have given a more masterly lesson?

The servant of God was not content with promoting the negative side of direction—the correcting of faults—but carefully considered also the positive aspect—the acquisition of virtues.

She labored hard to this end to carefully support grace in these young souls.

"I feel that it is necessary in direction," she wrote, "to absolutely forget one's own tastes and personal notions, and to guide souls—not by one's own way—but along the particular path which Jesus points out for them."

Therese acted in this objective way. With some, she instructed them in mortification and penance in union with Jesus, the immolated victim of calvary.

Teaching recollection to one daughter, Therese composed a prayer addressed to Christ standing silent before Herod, humbly asking for the virtue of which the novice had need.

There where the Holy Spirit manifested itself by secret touches, she dispensed the manna from heaven, abundantly sprinkled with sacred Scripture.

With the simplest souls, she started out on the life of silence and prayer of the holy family of Nazareth.

The Benjamin walked resolutely in the way of spiritual childhood, because she dreamed of only one thing—to give joy to the little Jesus.

One Christmas Eve, returning to her cell after midnight Mass, the young sister found a spinning top and a delightful letter.

"My well-beloved little spouse,

"I have something to say to you. Are you going to refuse Me? Oh! no, you love Me too much for that. Very well, I want to change the game; ninepins amuses Me very much, but now I want to play at spinning the top.[7]

"I am giving you one as a model; you see that it is not pretty on the outside; whoever does not know how to use it will kick it aside; but a child who notices it will jump with joy and say: 'What fun! it can go all day long without stopping.'"

"As for Me, the Little Jesus, I love you although you may not be beautiful; and I ask you always to walk so as to amuse Me. But in order to turn the top, one must whip it around! Very well, allow your Sisters to render you this service, and you will be grateful toward those who are the most diligent in quickening your pace.

"Then I will be very pleased with you, and I will take you away with Me on High and we will be able to play together without suffering.

Your little Brother,
Jesus"

Does one need to add that the author of this mysterious missive was none other than St. Therese of the Child Jesus?

By such a variety of ways the angelic mistress attained the unique end of her direction. Like the head of the family in the parable, she drew each day from her storehouse of treasures, distributing them according to the aptitudes of the souls confided to her care.

The firmness of her direction

Therese did not go about her task superficially.

No, she knew that the religious formation depended on early training of the novitiate. And since she was among souls who had left all to consecrate themselves to Christ, she did not intend to do things by halves.

Likewise, she did not hesitate to take vigorous measures in combating the faults of her novices. She tolerated no shortcomings in them and fought to her death to achieve this end. This twenty-year-old mistress possessed astonishing foresight.

"Since I have placed myself in the arms of Jesus," she confided, "I am like the watchman observing the enemy from the highest turret of a medieval citadel. Nothing escapes my notice."

As a simple novice, she fretted at seeing someone break the rule, saying to herself, "How I would like to reproach that Sister!"

Now that such was her duty, she changed her thinking. "I would rather receive a thousand reprimands than to give a single one!" she confessed.

Also, when she was in charge of the novices and she noticed some blunder of an older sister, Therese said to herself, "How happy I am that it is not a novice, and I don't have to reprimand her."

Then she would quickly excuse the fault and attribute the best of intentions to her.

Therese was convinced that to give effective fraternal correction, it be given reluctantly and as a matter of duty.

"In order for a reprimand to bear fruit," she declared, "it must cost something to the one who gives it; and it must be given without the least trace of passion."

This shows that the servant of God was confirmed in virtue and did not act out of vindictiveness or to please her superiors. Fortified by this interior calm, she braved the struggle to the point of being able to say, "I am just as at peace there as in prayer."

After a long discussion with a self-opinionated novice, she confided, "I have fought much; I am very tired; but I do not fear war because I want to do my duty at any cost."

She said to Mother Agnes of Jesus, "It is not necessary for goodness to degenerate into weakness. When one has given a just reprimand, she must let it rest there and not be moved to the point of worrying about having caused pain. To run after the afflicted one in order to console her is to make her worse rather than better. To let her to herself is to force her not to count upon the human side and to have recourse to God, to recognize her faults and to humble herself.

"Otherwise, she will become accustomed to being consoled after a well-deserved reproach, and she will act like a spoiled child who stamps its feet and cries knowing full well that its mother will come back to dry its tears."

Sometimes it was said to her, "If you want to get anything out of me, treat me gently; otherwise you'll gain nothing!"

But Therese reasoned that no one is a good judge in his own case. A child who submits to a painful operation does not refrain from loud cries, declaring that the remedy is worse than the disease. But after surgery when he feels cured, he is the first to thank the surgeon for his intervention.

"And so it is with souls," observed Therese, "they soon recognize that a little bitterness is preferable to sugar, and they are not afraid to acknowledge it."

She understood that direction is foremost a school of truth.

"With souls whom one is directing, one must be truthful and say what she thinks," she stated. "That is what I always do."

She did not approve of hypocritically "sitting on the fence." When she was chosen as arbitrator she gave her opinion frankly, whatever the protestations of the persons concerned.

"If they do not want to know the truth," she said, "they don't need to come looking for me. If I am not loved, too bad!"

Her pious direction

Aside from this vigorous manner of dealing with souls, Therese held a singular element of gentleness. Her severity was only a manifestation of her incomparable tenderness.

She mentioned this in her autobiography.

"I know, Mother, that your little lambs find me severe. They can say all that they wish; in reality, they feel that I love them with a very great love.

"No, there is no danger of my imitating the hireling who, seeing the wolf coming leaves the flock and flees.[8]

"I am ready to give my life for them, and my affection is so pure that I do not even want them to know it."

In her correspondence with Celine, we find an outline of her charity, ever in motion.

"I am a little hunting dog, and this title provides me with a good many cares because of the functions it requires of me: all day long I run after the game.

"The hunters—Reverend Mother and Mistress of Novices—are too big to slip into bushes while a little dog can intrude himself everywhere, and has a good nose besides! . . .

"So I watch by the side of my little rabbits; I do not wish to do them harm, but I ruffle them telling them that their fur is not smooth enough; at other times, their look resembles that of wild rabbits. Thus, I try to make them into something that the hunter wants: very simple little rabbits occupied only with the short grass which they must nibble."

These little rabbits were at times very tiring. But in the ardor of her devotion, the saintly mistress did not seem to notice. They interrupted her twenty times during an absorbing task. But she was at their service, always gracious and personable, ready to console or enlighten them, never refusing anyone, lavish without counting her time and labor.[9]

Occasionally, it seemed that her words fell on deaf ears. Even so, she slackened nothing in the exercise of her zeal.

"What does success matter! We always carry on no matter how hard the struggle," she said to Pauline. "Do not say, 'I can procure nothing for that soul; she does not understand, she is hopeless . . .' Oh! that would be cowardly! One must do her duty to the end!"

With what sweetness did she follow the inclination of her heart when, instead of reprimanding, she consoled and encouraged.

"I do not like to see holy souls suffer!" one of her companions mentioned to her one day.

"Oh! I do not feel that way," replied St. Therese of the Child Jesus. "I do not pity saints who suffer. I know that they have the strength to sustain them in their sufferings and in this way they give great glory to God.

"But those who are not saints and who do not know how to profit by their afflictions—Oh! I feel sorry for them! . . . I leave no stone unturned in order to console them and to comfort them."

During her last illness, noticing the care which the infirmary attendant took in choosing the softest linen for her, she observed, "This is how suffering souls are to be treated, even the most imperfect. Too often, they are hurt through want of attention and consideration; it is then that they are to be comforted and cared for with all our heart."

When one of her daughters came to make excuses for herself after having grieved her, she welcomed her with infinite gentleness.

"If you knew what I experienced!" she confided to one of her little repentant lambs. "If I, poor creature that I am, felt so much tenderness for you upon your return to me, what must take place in the Heart of the good God when we turn back to him!

"Yes, certainly, even quicker than I do it, He will forget all our iniquities and never again remember them. He will go further; He will love you even more than before your fall."[10]

Dying, she continued her apostolate. At times the novices took advantage of her good nature, not even waiting for her to finish her thanksgiving after Communion before consulting her. At first, she was saddened by it, then said, "I reflected that I should not desire more rest than Our Lord. When He fled into the desert, after His preaching, the people soon came to disturb His solitude. Come to me then as often as you wish. I must die with my weapons in hand, 'having on my lips the sword of the spirit which is the Word of God.' "[11]

Then thanking her on one of her last days for her inspiring counsel and edifying example, she answered simply, "It is the good God Who is pleased to instill in me those things which serve me well and which I communicate to others. 'The spirit of God blows where it will.' "[12]

Certainly, it was the spirit of love which spoke through her innocent mouth. "The Lord had given to her the gift of tongues and He has made waters of wisdom flow from her heart."[13]

Practical Application

If God has given the charge of souls to any of us, these are the lessons that we can draw from the example of that ideal mistress of novices, St. Therese of the Child Jesus.

I. It is important, first of all, that the direction be supernatural. To attain this, let us examine three principles.

(a) We must be souls of prayer, intimately united to our Lord. This is indispensible.

"The apostolate flows from the interior life; it is a chalice full of the God-Man poured out on souls," so precisely wrote Reverend Mateo. Now, how can one give what he does not possess?

(b) The second supernatural principle consists in not regarding oneself as the ambassador of God and in not changing the human nature which God clothed us in.

"As for me," St. Paul stressed, "I did not come with any show of oratory ... but simply to tell you what God had guaranteed."[14]

Let us act so that we can render the same testimony as St. Paul. That is to say, let us guide our subordinates in such a way that God will inspire us with the pure intention of approaching him without seeking personal satisfaction.

(c) The third condition is to seriously consider the supernatural worth of these souls which Jesus Christ has redeemed by his blood and in which the Holy Trinity has chosen to dwell through sanctifying grace.

These considerations will make us conscious of our responsibility. Either we make these spiritual trees bear divine fruit, or let them go uncultivated and unproductive through our negligence.

God will one day demand an account of our direction, whether to punish or to reward us. Recall the words of St. Therese of the Child Jesus.

"Ah! Souls would arrive at great sanctity if, from the beginning, they were well directed!"

How unfortunate if, through carelessness, we take from God a portion of the accidental glory that he counts on through our collaboration! This would cause us eternal regret.

II. May the example of St. Therese of the Child Jesus rouse us to intelligent direction.

(a) Certainly, with the help of divine wisdom, we will exercise ourselves in the discernment of spirits.[15]

The spirit of God is humility, simplicity, obedience, and peace. The spirit of the devil is pride, duplicity, rebellion, and trouble.

The devil sows cockle. We judge the seed by what it produces. Our opinion of the tree is determined by its fruits. Still, these fruits must be given the opportunity to mature. Perfection is not extemporaneous.

(b) A good director respects the originality of souls. To force them into a common mold is utopian. To treat them alike is nonsense.

There are no two souls exactly alike. Each differs by its personal modality and by the particular design that God has on each. Intelligent direction, then, consists in studying each soul intently and in adapting oneself to it according to the insights given us by grace.

It would be an error to a priori limit the time which one will give to each soul. To act this way would be like the unskilled gardener whom Therese called to account because he did not give more care to the greenhouse orchids than to the hardy flowers of the field. Some souls, like flowers, need more time and care than others.

Some persons, though imperfect, travel a clearly marked path with a pure conscience and a peaceful soul. They only need little signs to perform their duty.

Others—restless, agitated, lacking sunshine and support—become sickly and discouraged. To reject souls in distress under pretext that God will be their support is to tempt God.

The ordinary law of providence is not to intervene directly, but to make itself present to souls whose duty it is to direct them. It is their task then to sustain them in the purification through which the Lord lets them pass.

Still, certain souls believe they are being led by extraordinary ways. In these cases, the prudent director will caution them against diabolical and imaginative illusions.

Others are really privileged. But even with these it requires much tact to discern truth from falsity, to help them grow in divine grace by working attentively with them.

The director must give these souls room to open their hearts, at the same time carefully preventing the subtle poison of vanity from taking hold of them.

III. Lastly, St. Therese of the Child Jesus, this soul "strong as a diamond, tender as a mother,"[16] explicitly gave us by her example the rule of direction—strongly and sweetly.

Too much sweetness weakens. Too much vigor causes rebellion. The ideal is a well-balanced harmony of benevolence and strength.

Direction too complacent is as good as nothing. To universally approve but to ignore the pet shortcomings of spiritual children can be pleasant and sweet, but saints are not formed this way. The spirit of God is strong and true. One must speak the truth in season and out. This is the first blessing of direction. However, there is a time and manner to speak it.

One must be careful never to beat another to the ground when a light puff would be sufficient to dispel the difficulty.

It is praiseworthy to reprove souls, to enlighten them, to exact serious efforts of them, to correct them. But it must be done without rigidity, scorn, or arbitrary and excessive measures.

When we must correct, let us do it so that the one at fault knows that our reprimand is motivated by a supernatural love of neighbor and the desire to see him perfect. One can, one must, be firm without becoming hard.

"Each soul's make-up is such that she wants to be treated with kindness. When a fault is committed, strong characters are disgusted; weak characters are discouraged."[17]

Sometimes one must arm oneself with severity against rebellious spirits, give a little jolt to natures too apathetic. Even perfect souls can profit by a little rough handling. It is an occasion for them to accomplish heroic acts.

However, as a general rule, despite these advantages, abruptness is to be discouraged.

Therese experimented with the two systems, declaring that kindness gave her wings whereas fear oppressed her.

"You have not scolded me," she wrote to Mother Agnes of Jesus, "however much I deserved it. But in all circumstances, your gentleness spoke more to me than severe words."

Our Lord used a whip only once, and that was when he drove the merchants from the temple. Yet He said simply to those who were selling doves, "Take them away," because he did not wish to bruise anything he had created.

He was the world's greatest adversary of pride, avarice, hypocrisy. But in the face of weakness—little children, troublesome crowds, ignorant apostles, adulterous woman—He showed only mercy.

At the beginning of his abbotship, St. Bernard discouraged the majority of his monks by his rigorous and harsh code of rules. But in a vision, God made him understand his error. He changed his methods and from that time on, joy, peace, and expansion of soul reigned at Clairvaux. There souls joyously traveled the austere path of perfection.

Let us excel in benevolence while remaining firm and vigorous, and the Lord will make our apostolate fruitful by his grace.

COLLOQUY: With the strong and gentle Heart of Jesus Christ.

> The further I progress the more I find that gentleness is required in order to gain entrance into hearts and be sustained there, and to make them realize their duty without being severe with them. For after all, our Sisters are the ewes of Our Lord; He has permitted us, in leading them, to touch them with the shepherd's staff—but not to bruise them.
>
> *Letter of St. Jane de Chantal to a superior of the Visitation*

Notes

1. Ps. 119:141.
2. Ibid. 127:1.
3. *Counseils et Souvenirs*, p. 291.
4. In personal letters which have been publicized, Therese praised Celine highly for walking "the royal road of spiritual aridity."
5. *Vie de Ste. Therese de l'Enfant Jesus*, p. 282.
6. John 8:50.
7. The preceding year, this novice had "played ninepins." She pictured them as being all colors and sizes, in order to personify the souls that she wanted to reach. The ball in the game was her love.
8. John 16:12.
9. This patient affability in the exercise of her duty was given public mention by Benedict XIV when he spoke one day in praise of her sanctity.
10. *Conseils de Souvenirs*, p. 280.
11. Eph. 6:17.
12. John 3:8.

13. Eccles. 51:22; 50:27.
14. I Cor. 2:1.
15. Consult the *Spiritual Exercises* of St. Ignatius.
16. Intellectual portrait of Reverend Lacordaire drawn by his historian, Reverend Chocarne, O.P.
17. Reverend Schryvers, *Le Fondements de la Vie Spirituelle*.

Chapter Fourteen
Her Last Illness—Her Death

Jesus, for Your love
    My life I have exposed,
My hopes held high;
As in the eyes of men
    Forever fades the rose,
So I must die.

St. Therese of the Child Jesus

On July 30, 1897 St. Therese of the Child Jesus received the sacrament of the sick.

After her thanksgiving, she respectfully surveyed her emaciated hands which the holy oils of the sacrament had just purified and exclaimed delightedly, "The door of my bleak prison is ajar! I am filled with happiness especially since our Father Superior has assured me that my soul resembles today that of a little child after Baptism."

Her sisters gathered around her bed, she said to them, "O my Sisters, how happy I am! I know that I am going to die soon; I am sure of it now . . . I would like to have a beautiful death in order to please you; but do not grieve if I suffer much and if I do not show any sign of happiness at that time. Our Lord was a Victim of Love and you see what agony was His!"

It seems from these words that she had some sort of presentiment of her prolonged martyrdom.

As for the community, the nuns conjectured that her departure would be sweet and easy like a lily whose petals fall off gently in the scented silence of a summer's night.

The doctor, relying on his experience with consumptives, said this fallacy to her. "You will not suffer."

But she was to know all the physical and moral horrors of a double agony. One agonizing stage awaited her at Gethsemane before she definitely began her climb to calvary.

Toward the middle of August, the infirmary attendant noticed in Therese's features, ordinarily so peaceful, an unusual agonizing expression. She questioned her and received this answer.

"Ah! how necessary it is to pray for the dying!... if one only knew."

One night, she begged the sister watching her to throw some holy water on her bed, saying, "The devil is all around me; I do not see him, but I can feel him. He is tormenting me; he holds me with an iron hand in order to prevent me from grasping for the least comfort; he increases my discomfort so that I am despondent. And I cannot pray!... I can only look at the Blessed Virgin and say 'Jesus!'

"How necessary is the prayer at Compline: 'Procul recedant somnia, et noctium phantasmata!'—Deliver us from the dreams and from the phantoms of the night. I am experiencing something mysterious. I am not suffering for myself but for another soul, and the devil does not want that."

The infirmary attendant lit a blessed candle, and the spirit of darkness fled, never returning.[1]

The angelic nun had emerged victorious from this infernal hand-to-hand combat, but the most complete aridity and sense of helplessness continued to make her languish.

When she contemplated the marvelous blue heavens by a partly opened window, her sisters thought she was joyfully pondering her future dwelling place. Nothing of the sort.

She confided to Mother Agnes of Jesus, "The Sisters do not

know what I suffer! Looking up there, I reflect only on the beauty of the material sky. The other is closed to me more and more."

Yet her lively faith quickened on certain days by the eucharistic coming of Jesus. The cloisters were then decorated with flowers, the sun shone through them brightly, the birds chirped playfully in the monastery courtyard, and the procession of nuns in their black veils and white mantles preceded the priest chanting the miserere.

Pale on her narrow bed, the little virgin of Jesus, silent and recollected, waited for her beloved.

A heavenly calm and purity reigned in the infirmary. Usually so full of suffering, this place was changed from daybreak into a little bit of heavenly splendor. Was not Jesus coming? Oh, what an exquisite meeting!

Sr. Marie of the Eucharist,[2] who became the echo of her intimate aspirations, sweetly sang these verses which Therese had composed during the night.

> You Who know my extreme littleness above,
>   You do not mind coming down to me;
> Come to my heart, O Love that I love,
>   Come to my heart, it longs so for Thee.

She was enraptured by this spiritual consolation. From August 17, her vomiting became so frequent that it was necessary to deprive her of the blessed sacrament.

Frightening bouts of choking lasted for hours at a time. Then she would sign softly, "O my God, have pity on me, You Who are so good!"

When her breathing became labored, she groaned intermittently. "I am suffering! I am suffering!" Then she would reproach herself for complaining.

"Each time that I say: 'I am suffering,' you answer 'so much the better!'" she charged her faithful attendant. "That's what I want to say to complete my thought, but I do not always have the strength to do it."

Amazed, her physician said, "I have never seen this kind of consumption. It is frightful what this young religious can endure—and with what patience. She is an angel!"

When told what the doctor had said, Therese answered simply, "Can a little victim of love find 'frightful' what her Spouse sends her? The truth is that I am suffering only as much as I am able to bear."

With an inexpressible serenity, she confided to Mother Agnes of Jesus. "I am like a very little child; at times, I have not a single thought except that of a simple acquiescence to all that God wishes, suffering minute by minute what He sends me without preoccupying myself with the future.

"I rejoice at the thought of death because it is the expression of the Will of God for me. I do not desire death more than life. My nature prefers death; but if I had a choice, I would choose neither; it is only what God does that I love,"[3]

She was asked, "Are you not afraid of death now that you see yourself so near it?"

"Ah! less and less."

"Are you not afraid of the 'thief?' "[4] persisted her sister. "This time he is at the door."

"No, He is not at the door; He has come in. But why do you ask me that, Little Mother—if I am afraid of the 'thief'? Do you think that I can be afraid of Someone I love so much? Death is not a phantom, a horrible spectre like it is pictured. It is written in the catechism that death is the separation of body and soul; it is only that! Then, why would I dread a separation which will unite me forever to God?"

"Oh! what joy to see myself falling into decay!" she exclaimed at another time, looking at her emaciated arms.

And as Sr. Marie of the Sacred Heart said to her sadly, "How grieved we shall be after your death!"

Therese came back at her playfully: "Oh! no, you will see: It will be like a shower of roses."

These were not the only rays of sunshine. At times St. Therese of the Child Jesus felt that God, though trying her, was watching her tenderly.

For example, one evening during the great silence her attendant brought her a foot warmer and painted her chest with tincture of iodine.

Therese was feverish and burning with thirst. Submitting to these treatments, she could not keep from telling our Lord, "My Jesus, You see it; I am burning up and they still keep bringing me these hot things! ah! if only I had instead just half a glass of water, how very comforting it would be. O my God, Your little child is so thirsty! But she is happy anyhow to be without things that are necessary in order to be more like You and to save souls."

The attendant left. Therese thought that she would not see her again until the next day, but she returned a few minutes later carrying a refreshing drink.

"I happened to think that you might be thirsty," she said. "From now on, I'll see that you get this little refreshment every night."

The invalid looked at her dumbfounded. As soon as she was alone she burst into tears.

"Ah! how good Jesus is!" she said to herself, "how easily His Heart is touched!"

By the partially opened window of the infirmary which looked out on the shaded groves of the garden, a little robin sometimes perched in the sunshine. It ventured inquisitively to Therese's bed, doing dozens of little tricks for her.

Does this charming incident not remind one of the stories of St. Francis who, because of his unique sancitity, was able to exercise influence over animals?

But intense sufferings followed these moments of joy for the invalid. One morning, she awoke shuddering and experienced the overwhelming oppression which weighs one down at the prospect of dissolution.

"I am afraid of fearing death!" she explained afterward.

"Whatever will happen to me after death does not disturb me; I merely ask myself with a certain degree of anguish: 'What is this mysterious separation of body and soul?' But immediately I abandon myself to God."

Another time, pointing through the window to a dark corner of the garden, she said to Mother Agnes of Jesus, "Do you see over there beside the chestnut trees—that gap where you can't distinguish anything? It is in the same kind of abyss as I am in body and soul. What darkness! But through it all I am in peace."[5]

When the prioress came to visit, Therese said, "Mother, I would like to confide to you the state of my soul, but I cannot do it; I am too moved at this moment."

In the evening, she sent her this note written with a trembling hand.

> O my God, how good You are towards the little victim of Your Merciful love. Even now that You add exterior suffering to the trials of my soul I can only say: 'the agonies of death have surrounded me;' but I cry out trustingly: 'I have gone down into the valley of the shadows of death; yet, I fear no evil because You are with me, Lord!'[6]

On September 24, the day which the servant of God observed her anniversary of the taking of the veil, Mother Agnes of Jesus had the Mass celebrated that day for this intention. When Therese learned of this she thanked her.

"What a pity!" her little mother said to her. "It does not comfort you!"

"Is it for my comfort that Mass was said?"

"It's for your good."

"My good . . . no doubt it's to suffer?"[7]

After a particularly painful day, she confided to Mother Agnes of Jesus, "This afternoon, I heard the answer someone gave to a Sister who asked how I was: 'she is very tired.' Then I thought: It is true; so very true! Yes, I am like a tired and weary traveller who collapses when she arrives at the end of her journey."

Another time, alluding to the parable of the good samaritan, she said, "I am like this poor no-account traveller: half living, half dead!"

Indeed, acute pains, deep wounds, high fever, and a state of general exhaustion added to continual sufferings of soul contributed to making the invalid a martyr.

"Oh! Mother," she cried out one day, "what will become of me if the good God does not give me strength? I can no longer do it on my own. No one knows what it is to suffer like this. No, he must feel it."

It was the desperate cry of nature. Listen to grace coming to the fore.

"I am suffering much," she confided, "but am I not suffering well? That is the important thing."

Anxious to "suffer well," she abstained from applying remedies to her ailments.

"Oh, how my shoulder pains me; if only you knew!" she groaned one day.

"We'll put some padding on it."

"No, it is not necessary to remove my little cross."

One day, Mother Agnes of Jesus praying on her knees beside her bed, Therese said to her, "You are sad, Mother, why?"

"Because you are suffering so much."

"Yes, but with what peace! what peace!"

From September 25 she became excessively weak, soon reduced to where she could no longer even stir by herself. Someone speaking at her bedside, even in a low voice, disturbed her. Fever and oppression imposed on her a painful silence, broken by coughing fits.

On one of her last nights, the attendant (Sr. Genevieve of the Holy Face, who slept in an adjoining room ready to answer her slightest call) came into the infirmary and saw Therese with her hands joined, her eyes gazing heavenward.

"Why are you doing this?" she asked. "You must try to sleep."

"I cannot sleep; and that's when I pray."

"And what are you saying to Jesus?"

"I am not saying anything to Him; I love Him."[8]

Another time, the sister surprised Therese. Crucifix in hand, her fingers moved lovingly over the lacerated brow and bruised limbs of the Savior.

"What are you doing there?"

"I am taking His nails out and removing His crown of thorns."[9]

Two days before her death, Therese, then in the company of Celine, distinctly heard wings rustling in the garden. A little later a turtledove perched itself on the window sill and began to coo.

The two sisters were tenderly moved by this, remembering the invitation in the Song of Songs. "The song of the turtledove is heard in our land; come, then, my lovely one, come, for see, winter is passed."[10]

Yes, the approach of the bridegroom was near.

On September 29, from early morning a mournful cry seemed to foretell the inevitable end.

Toward noon, the dying nun said to her prioress, "Mother, is this the agony? What can I do to die?"

Mother Mary of Gonzaga found nothing more appropriate than to read to her the office of St. Michael and the prayers for the dying, that admirable liturgical ritual with which Holy Mother Church leads her children to the brink of eternity.

When the demons were mentioned, Therese made a childish gesture as if to threaten them and exclaimed smiling, "Oh! Oh!" in a tone which meant, "I'm not afraid of them."

After Dr. Corniere's visit, St. Therese of the Child Jesus asked, "Is it today, Mother?"

"Yes," the prioress answered.

A few hours later, a new crisis followed which ordinarily precedes the final struggle of a dying person.

"I can't take anymore! ah! pray for me! If only you knew!" she lamented.

After the hour of matins, she folded her hands and in a soft and plaintive voice, she repeated, "Yes, my God, yes! yes! I am so very willing."

"Are you suffering a great deal?" asked Mother Mary of Gonzaga.

"No, Mother, not a great deal, but much, much . . . just what I am able to bear."

She begged to be left alone at night, but the prioress would not consent. Sr. Marie of the Sacred Heart and Sr. Genevieve of the Holy Face shared watching her.

As Celine fondly entreated her for one word of farewell, Therese responded, "I have said everything . . . all is accomplished! It is only love that counts."

Contrary to her sisters' expectations, the holy invalid lived through the night. But the next day, September 30, was to be the last day of her exile here below. The blessed dawn of her birth into heaven, of that dies natalis so much desired, was at last here.

From morning on, she was racked with unspeakable suffering. Looking at the virgin of the smile placed opposite her bed, she said, "Oh! I have prayed to her with such fervor! But it is pure agony, without one drop of consolation."

She went through that day without a moment of respite. Fevered, she sat up on her bed—something she had not been able to do for a long time.

"See what strength I have today," she said. "No, I'm not going to die. Perhaps I still have another month. I no longer believe that death is for me; I believe only that there is more suffering! And tomorrow it will be still worse."

This unnatural strength was a last spurt of her energy struggling against the terrors of dissolution.

"Ah!" she sighed, "if this is the agony, what must death be like?" Then she added, surprised that such a state of anguish could be reached.

"The chalice is filled to the brim! But God is not going to abandon me. He has never abandoned me . . . yes, my God . . . all that You will, but have pity on me!"

Then turning toward her sisters, she begged them, "Little Sisters, pray for me."

About three o'clock, recalling the death of Christ, she extended her arms in the form of a cross, and Mother Mary of Gonzaga placed on her coverlet an image of Our Lady of Mt. Carmel.

She looked at it piously and said, "Oh, Mother, present me very quickly to the Blessed Virgin. Prepare me to die well."

The prioress answered her, saying, "My child, you are all prepared to appear before God because you have always understood the virtue of humility."

The fervent nun thought, then said, "Yes, I have never sought anything but the truth. Yes, I have understood humility of heart." Thinking of her spiritual testament,—her autobiography,—which was only awaiting her death in order to begin its influence on the world, she added, "Everything that I have written about my desires for suffering, Oh! it is so true! I do not regret having given myself up to love."

From this moment, observed one sister, "It seemed that it was no longer she who was suffering! Many times, looking at her, I thought of the martyrs being delivered to the executioners, yet animated by a divine strength."

A little later, she choked and said, "I cannot breathe, I cannot die." Then she resigned herself. "But I wish to suffer still more." Speaking as if to herself, she added, "I would never have believed that it was possible to suffer so much. I can only explain it by the ardent desires which I have had to save souls."

Looking back over her life, engulfed by the preference of the all-powerful, she said, "Since my many little desires have been realized . . . then, the greatest of them, to die of love, must be it."

Toward five o'clock, Mother Agnes of Jesus was alone with the dying nun during prayer when she suddenly saw the death mask come over her features. This time it was the real agony. A hasty ringing of the bell called the community to the infirmary.

As soon as she saw the sisters coming, Therese gave each a smile of gratitude. Then, conscious of the last moments, she became absorbed in her crucifix.

For two more hours a terrible rattle tore at her chest. Her pallid face, purple hands, already cold and numb feet, all indicated the end. She was trembling all over and sweat soon soaked the covers and mattress. To get her breath, she moaned laboriously.

Desiring to comfort her, Sr. Genevieve of the Holy Face, who was at her post in the infirmary until the end, leaned over her dying sister and moistened her dry lips with a small piece of ice. Therese, moved by this last delicate attention, smiled at her little Celine with an infinite tenderness.

Toward seven o'clock, seeing no change in her condition, the mother prioress dismissed the community for the time being. Turning to her, Therese murmured disappointedly, "Mother, isn't this the agony yet? Am I not going to die?"

"Yes, my child, it is the agony; but perhaps God wants to prolong it for a few hours yet."

"Very well! let it continue! . . . let it continue! . . . oh! I would not wish to suffer less." Then, looking at her crucifix, she said, "Oh! I love Him! . . . My God . . . I . . . love . . . You!"

Those were her last words.

Suddenly, as if an invisible arrow had struck her square in the heart, she fell back onto her bed, her head inclined to the right.

Seeing that this was the end, the prioress called the community back quickly. "Open all the doors," she said.

"Those words had a solemn ring to them at that moment," observed Mother Agnes of Jesus, "and I thought that in heaven the Lord was saying the same thing to His angels."

Hardly had the sisters knelt, before the dying Therese sat up straight again as if called by a mysterious voice. Her suffering face became transfigured and instantly took on the velvety appearance of a flower just as when she had been in good health.

By certain movements of her head, they concluded that she was undergoing a sort of mystical assault, as if a stroke of the divine conqueror had severed the last ties of her soul from her body. At the same time the ecstatic eyes of the saint, fixed on high, seemed captivated by a marvelous apparition, the sight of which transported her out of this world.

What did she see? The queen of angels? the gate of heaven?

her heavenly mother who came to introduce her into the
heavenly Jerusalem? or better still, Jesus himself?—this unseen
and so ardently loved spouse who was taking her into his arms
with a divine smile: "Veni Sponsa Christi! . . . Come Spouse of
Christ!" Unfathomable enigma of which eternity will reveal the
mystery.

Therese's motionless gaze lasted for the space of a credo, then
her breathing stopped, the light in her beautiful eyes gone out.
The angel had spread out her wings. Little Therese was dead.

In death, Therese preserved a heavenly smile, a ravishing
beauty. Her folded hands clasped her crucifix so tightly that it
was necessary to pry them loose to prepare her for burial.

Her two older sisters, assisted by an old infirmary attendant,
reverentially performed this last duty. Her virginal remains appeared so young that she could have passed for twelve or thir-
teen. She was truly a little child who had gone to sleep in the
arms of the Lord.

When the servant of God was laid out in choir, according to
custom, her face took on a majestic expression. She looked like a
queen lulled to sleep in the splendor of her regal throne.

Miraculous events occurred in the monastery from the day
after her death. And her holy remains stayed supple until her
burial, October 4.

A retinue of priests and faithful escorted her to her last resting
place, forming the simple but glorious vanguard of the ideal nun
whose posthumous fame was not to have tarried in conquering
the universe.

Practical Application

St. Therese of the Child Jesus was one of those wise virgins
who, labored hard to maintain the lamp of divine love in her
heart by the oil of good works.

When, in the silence of an autumn night, this plaintive summons echoed in her ears, "The Spouse is coming, go out to meet

Him," she entered the banquet hall with a quiet conscience and a soul overflowing with merits and grace.

Suppose that this last summons was addressed to us at this moment. Would we answer it with the same assurance?

Is not the lamp, symbolizing our love for God, flickering and ready to go out? Do we have time to run and buy the oil from those who sell it?[11] That is to say, to go to the priest who, through absolution, gives back the life of grace to souls and prepares them through the sacrament of the sick for the last voyage.

Our death may be sudden, terrible. And who knows if we may hear the gates of heaven close relentlessly before us with these severe words from the bridegroom, "Truly, I say, I do not know you."[12]

We will be woefully pitied, but not excused. The Son of God is incarnate. He has taught the world truth. He has ratified it by his miracles and affirmed it at the cost of his life. He rose again on the third day, and he ascended into heaven in the presence of five hundred witnesses. Why are we so obstinate in believing?

Through baptism, God has given us the initial gift of sanctifying grace. It is developed through the other sacraments and the actual graces which we call into action at each moment. Why do we not hope?

Jesus Christ died on the cross in order to redeem us, and everyday on our altars his immolation is renewed in us in a mystical manner. Why do we not love?

If we wish, He will nourish us each morning with his body thereby making us stand strong. Why have we been so weak and sinful?

The Church—through its ministers, instructs—warns and reprimands us. Why have we remained deaf and inattentive?

We are foolish, superficial, insensitive virgins, absorbed in earthly trifles as if such things were essential and rooted in us forever.

The prophetic hour has struck for us. The son of man has

warned us that he will come unexpectedly as a thief, and he is going to keep his word.

"For mercy's sake, Lord, have pity on us, give us a little respite; give us time to be reconciled to You and to our neighbor, time to perform a few good works that may not be defiled by self-love, time to chastise our bodies and to bring them into subjection[13] so as to be spared eternal fire or purgatory which awaits us."

Those of us who read these lines are living today, but may be dead tomorrow. Let us thank the Lord for his mercy in granting us a delay. Let us profit by it, becoming like the apostles and saints, raising ourselves. Let us correct our faults, love God with all our might, so that when the final accounts are settled we will hear the voice of the divine master address us in these comforting words, "Well done, good and faithful servant. I will trust you with greater things; come and share your Master's happiness!"[14]

COLLOQUY: With St. Therese of the Child Jesus

Yes, after the example of Therese, we will die the death of the just, and may our end resemble hers.

Notes

1. *Story of a Soul*, Ch. 12.
2. Her cousin, Marie Guerin.
3. *Summarium of 1919*, p. 865.
4. Allusion to that passage in the gospel wherein our Lord is compared to a thief who comes to take souls when they least expect it.
5. *Summarium of 1919*, p. 925.
6. Ibid., p. 865.
7. Ibid., p. 929.
8. *Summarium of 1919*, p. 843.

9. *Sainte Therese de l'Enfant Jesus*, p. 388.
10. Song of Songs 2:12.
11. Matt. 25:9–10.
12. Ibid., 25:12.
13. I Cor. 9:27.
14. Matt. 25:21.

Epilogue

I am a daughter of the Church!
My glory will be the reflection
    Which will shine forth from the
    face of my Mother!
                                        St. Therese of the Child Jesus

Some time after the death of Therese, when she began to let her "showers of roses" fall, the Assistant General of the Society of Jesus in Rome reflected, "The glory of Therese keeps rising! But she is still far from her zenith. This little saint will perform such marvels here below of which these splendid days will be only a prelude. In the Kingdom of Heaven, this child has the palm of victory, and she will let it be seen!"

This priest had the right idea. From that time the spread of *The Story of a Soul* was truly prodigious and, according to a prediction of the saint of Lisieux to one of her intimate companions, "the shower of roses had turned into a torrent."

Supplications, graced with thousands of signatures, swamped the Vatican imploring the Sovereign Pontiffs to hasten this process so universally extolled.

By an exception to the prudent legislation of the Church, His Holiness Benedict XV exempted her from the fifty-year delay imposed by Benedict XIV from the death of a servant of God to the judicial beginnings of their beatification process.

Because of this exemption, Therese, dispenser of roses and always gracious in her simplicity, was placed on the altars on April 29, 1923.

Here this star, scarcely sparkling in the morning mist, twenty-five years later became a dazzling meteor whose splendor yet illuminates the whole house of the Lord.

Let us pause a moment in contemplation before the pinnacle of her glory, the zenith of her marvelous radiance.

On that radiant Sunday, May 17, 1925, which marked the definitive glory of Therese, a crowd of more than one hundred fifty thousand pilgrims thronged into St. Peter's basilica.

At the entrance to the Vatican, a custom unanimously observed, all windows of the old quarter of the borgo were decked with flags and decorated with roses. In the interior of the basilica, gigantic bouquets of light splashed to the top of the electric candelabra, rivaling the solar brightness which profusely radiated the nave through the immense archways.

On either side of the confessional, in the glory of Bernini, two great paintings represented the miracles worked through the intercession of the new saint in favor of Marie Pellemans of Brussels and Sr. Gabrielle Trimusi, a religious sister from Parma.

Later the procession gathered in the Sistine Chapel and the spacious apartments of the pontifical palace. The bells rang joyously, and the procession crossed the threshold of St. Peter's moving forward between two rows of palatine guards.

Bright banners and crosses went with the crowd. The march was made up of thirty-three cardinals, two hundred archbishops and bishops preceded by numerous clergy. While the standard of Therese passed through the basilica, there were loud acclamations and moving supplications. When the Holy Father came through on the sedilia in his red cape and white skullcap, applause surged like thunder under the golden domes.

It was ten thirty when Monsignor Sebastiani, secretary to the Pope, pronounced the solemn invitation. "Assurgite igitur: Petrus per Pium locuturus est: All rise. Peter is going to speak through the mouth of Pius."

Before standing cardinals and bishops, His Holiness Pius XI, seated with his miter on his head, pronounced the ritual formula, "declaring SAINT, the Blessed Therese of the Child Jesus and determining that each year on the day of her birth into heaven, that is, on September 30, her memory be piously recalled by the universal Church."[1]

After the Gospel, the Holy Father brought out in a touching address the characteristic note of the sanctity of Therese— spiritual childhood. Ending his homily with the desire that a multitude of souls walk henceforth in the footsteps of the little child of Lisieux, a few roses became detached from one of the candelabras and fell gently at the pontiff's side.

That first canonization of the holy year ended in splendid glory. For the first time in half a century,[2] the fascinated Romans saw the magical conflagration of St. Peter's under the starry sky. Thousands of lights glittered from the immense basilica.

Before the enchanting allegory of this spectacle, more than one obscure Christian—lost in the crowd of five hundred thousand milling around—felt a thrill in his heart and cried out to himself, "O Church of Christ! O my well-beloved, you alone are beautiful, you alone are invincible.

"You alone stood undisturbed for twenty centuries in peaceful majesty like an eternal sphinx against which weak enemies took their turns in venting their powerless rage.

"You alone are the depository of truth. Outside of you, there is only darkness and emptiness.

"You alone set your course noiselessly on the proud sea of time with the splendor of a vessel of light which rows towards the serene shores of eternity.

"How happy are your children! How happy are those who nurse at your breast! They possess the pledge and the first fruits of the true life.

"The glory that the world affords its partisans is as unstable and ephemeral as smoke in the wind; but that which you bestow, oh, well-beloved Spouse of Christ, is truth and immortality.

"Why certainly, little Therese of Lisieux has chosen the better part of which she herself wrote, 'I am a daughter of the Church! My glory will be the reflection which will shine forth from the face of my Mother.'

"You have taken her at her word, Oh, Church of God, and you have condescended toward your little Carmelite daughter. You have lifted her up in your strong arms to face the world, and with a maternal kiss you have told her in canonizing her, 'On this day, oh my little one, I place on your head a sparkling diadem, I have made a covenant with you and you have become mine.'

"You have acquired a dazzling beauty; and you rose to be a queen and henceforth your name will be extolled among nations[3] because I, the Church, will it."

Notes

1. In America, her feast is celebrated on October 1.
2. A personal desire of the Sovereign Pontiff had motivated this exterior illumination which had not been seen since 1870.
3. Ez. 16:5 ff.

Act of Oblation to Merciful Love

Offering of myself as a
Victim of Holocaust to
God's Merciful Love.

O my God! O Most Blessed Trinity! I want to love You and to make You loved—to labor for the glory of Holy Church by saving souls on earth and delivering those suffering in purgatory. I desire to accomplish Your Will perfectly and to reach that degree of glory which You have prepared for me in Your Kingdom. In a word, I want to be a saint but knowing my helplessness, I beg You, my God, to be Yourself my sanctity.

Since You have loved me so much as to give me Your Only-Begotten Son to be my Savior and my Spouse, the infinite treasures of His merits are mine. Gladly do I offer them to You, and I beg You to look at me only through the eyes of Jesus, and in His Heart burning with love.

Moreover, I offer You all the merits of the Saints both in Heaven and on earth together with their acts of love and those of the holy Angels.

Finally, I offer You, O Blessed Trinity! the love and the merits of the Blessed Virgin, my dear Mother. It is to her that I commit this oblation, begging her to present it to You.

Her Divine Son, my Beloved Spouse, during the days He spent on earth, said to us: "If you ask the Father anything in My Name, He will give it to you." I am certain then that you will fulfill my longing; I know, O my God! that the more You wish to give, the more You make us desire. In my heart I feel boundless desires, and with confidence I beg You to take possession of my soul. I cannot receive You in Holy Communion as often as I desire; but, O Lord, are You not all-powerful? Remain in me as in a tabernacle and never separate Yourself from Your little Victim.

I long to console You for the ingratitude of sinners, and I beg of You to take away from me all liberty to sin. If I should some-times fall through weakness, may Your divine glance cleanse my soul immediately and consume all my imperfections as fire transforms all things into itself.

I thank You, O my God, for all the graces You have given me: especially for having purified me in the crucible of suffering. On Judgment Day, I will look upon You with joy as You carry the sceptre of the Cross. Since You have deigned to give me a share of this precious Cross, I hope to resemble You in Paradise and see Your Sacred Wounds shine on my glorified body.

After earth's exile, I trust that I will possess You in our Father's House; but I do not seek to lay up treasures for Heaven. I want to work for Your Love alone with the sole purpose of pleasing You, of consoling Your Sacred Heart, and of saving souls who will love You for all eternity.

In the evening of this life, I shall stand before You with empty hands because I do not ask You, my God, to take account of my works. All justice appears blemished in Your eyes. Therefore, I wish to be clothed with Your own Justice and to receive from Your Love the eternal gift of Yourself. I desire no other throne, no other crown but You, O my Beloved! In Your eyes, time is nothing—"One day is a thousand years." You can then in a single moment prepare me to appear before You.

So that my life may be one act of perfect love, I offer myself as a Victim of Holocaust to Your Merciful Love, begging You to consume me without ceasing, allowing the waves of infinite ten-derness which are shut up within You to overflow into my soul so that I may become a martyr of divine love, O my God!

May this martyrdom, after having prepared me to appear before You, finally cause me to die, and may my soul take its flight without delay into the eternal embrace of Your Merciful Love.

I desire, O my Well-Beloved, with each beat of my heart, to renew this offering an infinite number of times until, the shadows having vanished, I can tell You again of my love, face to face, eternally!

Marie Francoise Therese of the Child Jesus
and the Holy Face
June 9, 1895

Little Flower's Days of Grace

Birth	January 2, 1873
Baptism	January 4, 1873
The smile of our Lady	May 10, 1883
First Holy Communion	May 8, 1884
Confirmation	June 14, 1884
Conversion—her "Christmas Grace"	December 25, 1886
Audience with Leo XIII	November 20, 1887
Entrance into Carmel	April 8, 1888
Taking of the habit	January 10, 1889
Profession	September 8, 1890
Taking of the veil	September 24, 1890
Act of oblation to merciful love	June 9, 1895
Death	September 30, 1897
Cause of beatification introduced in Rome	June 9, 1914
Beatification	April 29, 1923
Canonization	May 17, 1925
Declared patroness of the missions	December 14, 1927